Mastering Project Management:
A Practical Guide to Success

Mariam AlKuwaiti

INDIA • SINGAPORE • MALAYSIA

ISBN 979-8-89929-356-6

Contents

Introduction

In today's rapidly evolving business landscape, project management has emerged as an indispensable discipline, essential for steering organizations towards achieving their strategic goals. Whether launching a new product, implementing cutting-edge technologies, or managing complex organizational changes, effective project management serves as the backbone of successful execution. This book, "Mastering Project Management: A Practical Guide to Success," is crafted to equip both aspiring and seasoned project managers with the essential tools, methodologies, and insights needed to navigate the multifaceted challenges of contemporary projects.

The essence of successful project management lies in its ability to harmonize diverse elements—people, processes, and technology—into a cohesive and efficient whole. This requires not only technical acumen but also a deep understanding of human dynamics, strategic thinking, and adaptive leadership. Throughout this guide, you will find a rich tapestry of practical advice, strategic frameworks, and real-world examples designed to enhance your project management acumen.

This book delves into the core principles that underpin project management success, from initiating and planning to executing, monitoring, and closing. It emphasizes the importance of setting clear objectives, managing scope, identifying risks, and ensuring quality, all while maintaining a focus on stakeholder engagement and communication. Each chapter is meticulously structured to provide actionable insights, empowering you to apply best practices and innovative approaches tailored to your unique project environments.

Moreover, "Mastering Project Management" recognizes the significance of adapting to the digital age's demands, where agility and flexibility are paramount. It explores contemporary methodologies such as Agile, Lean, and hybrid models, encouraging you to adopt a mindset of continuous improvement and resilience.

Whether you are a novice eager to embark on your project management career or a seasoned professional seeking to refine your skills, this book offers a comprehensive roadmap to mastering the art and science of project management. Let this guide be your companion in navigating the complexities of modern projects, driving results that not only meet but exceed expectations. Welcome to a journey of professional growth, where mastery of project management becomes a catalyst for success in any industry.

Chapter 1:

Introduction to Project Management

Defining Project Management

Project management is a multifaceted discipline that encompasses a structured approach to planning, executing, and overseeing initiatives to achieve specific goals within defined parameters. It is a field that synthesizes knowledge areas, methodologies, and tools to ensure projects are completed efficiently, effectively, and within the constraints of time, cost, and quality.

At its core, project management involves the application of knowledge, skills, tools, and techniques to project activities to meet project requirements. This process is delineated into several phases, typically initiation, planning, execution, monitoring, and closing. Each phase plays a crucial role in steering the project to its successful completion.

The initiation phase is where the project is formally authorized. This involves defining the project at a high level, identifying stakeholders, and establishing the project's objectives and feasibility. A project charter is often developed during this phase, outlining the project's scope, objectives, and stakeholders.

Following initiation, the planning phase is where detailed project plans are developed. This phase involves the creation of comprehensive documents that guide the project team in executing the project. Key components of the planning phase include scope management, schedule development, cost estimation, quality planning, and risk management. These elements are crucial as they provide a roadmap for the project team and establish baselines against which project performance can be measured.

The execution phase is where project plans are put into action. This phase involves coordinating people and resources, as well as integrating and performing the activities of the project in accordance with the project management plan. The execution phase is often the longest in terms of duration, requiring effective communication, stakeholder engagement, and problem-solving skills to ensure the project stays on track.

Monitoring and controlling processes occur concurrently with execution to track, review, and regulate project performance. This phase involves measuring project performance using appropriate tools and techniques, and identifying any areas where changes to the plan are required. Variance analysis, performance reviews, and risk audits are common practices during this phase to ensure alignment with project objectives.

The closing phase marks the formal completion of the project. This phase involves finalizing all activities, completing project documentation, obtaining formal acceptance from stakeholders, and conducting lessons learned sessions. The closing phase ensures that the project is concluded in an orderly manner and that all deliverables meet the predefined acceptance criteria.

Project management is not a static field; it evolves continuously with advancements in technology, methodologies, and organizational practices. Agile, lean, and hybrid approaches are increasingly adopted to enhance flexibility and responsiveness in project delivery. These methodologies emphasize iterative development, continuous feedback, and adaptive planning, aligning project management practices with the dynamic nature of modern business environments.

In conclusion, project management is an indispensable discipline that enables organizations to achieve strategic objectives through structured and methodical approaches. It requires a blend of technical acumen, interpersonal skills, and strategic vision to navigate the complexities of diverse projects and deliver tangible results. As businesses strive for innovation and efficiency, the role of project management becomes ever more critical in steering projects to success.

History and Evolution

Project management, as a formal discipline, has its roots deeply embedded in the industrial age, where large-scale operations and complex undertakings necessitated a structured approach to planning, executing, and overseeing projects. The inception of modern project management can be traced back to the late 19th and early 20th centuries, coinciding with the rise of large-scale engineering projects such as the construction of the transcontinental railroad and the Panama Canal.

The early 20th century saw the development of key project management concepts and methodologies that remain fundamental today. One of the pioneering contributions was the Gantt chart, introduced by Henry L. Gantt in the 1910s. This visual tool allowed for the graphical representation of schedules, enabling project managers to track progress effectively and allocate resources efficiently.

Simultaneously, Frederick W. Taylor's principles of scientific management laid the groundwork for systematic project planning and execution. His emphasis on time and motion studies led to the optimization of labor and processes, significantly influencing project management practices. Taylor's work highlighted the importance of efficiency and productivity, principles that continue to underpin modern project management.

The post-World War II era marked a significant shift in project management as industries expanded and technological advancements accelerated. The development of the Critical Path Method (CPM) by DuPont and the Program Evaluation Review Technique (PERT) by the United States Navy in the late 1950s revolutionized project scheduling and risk management. CPM provided a mathematical approach to scheduling, while PERT introduced statistical techniques for managing uncertainty in project timelines.

As industries diversified and projects became increasingly multifaceted, the 1960s and 1970s witnessed the emergence of formalized project management organizations and standards. The establishment of the Project Management Institute (PMI) in 1969 was a landmark event, providing a professional framework and a body of knowledge that unified project managers globally. The PMI's development of the Project Management Body of Knowledge (PMBOK) Guide standardized practices and terminology, fostering consistency across the profession.

The advent of digital technology in the late 20th and early 21st centuries further transformed project management. Software tools such as Microsoft Project and Primavera facilitated detailed planning, scheduling, and resource allocation, enhancing the precision and efficiency of project management processes. The rise of Agile methodologies in the software industry introduced a paradigm shift, emphasizing flexibility, collaboration, and iterative development. Agile's iterative cycles and adaptability have since been adopted across various sectors, reflecting a broader trend towards dynamic and responsive project management.

In recent years, project management has continued to evolve in response to globalization, technological innovation, and the increasing complexity of projects. Emerging trends such as virtual project management, sustainability considerations, and data-driven decision-making are shaping the future of the discipline. As organizations face unprecedented challenges and opportunities, project management remains a critical enabler of strategic objectives, facilitating the successful delivery of projects in an ever-changing landscape.

Throughout its history, project management has demonstrated a remarkable capacity for adaptation and innovation, continually refining its methodologies to meet the demands of a complex world. This evolution underscores the discipline's enduring relevance and its pivotal role in driving organizational success across diverse domains.

Importance in Modern Business

Project management has emerged as an integral component of contemporary business strategies, serving as a linchpin in the orchestration of complex initiatives and the realization of organizational objectives. In an era characterized by rapid technological advancements and dynamic market conditions, the ability to manage projects efficiently is crucial for maintaining competitive advantage and ensuring sustainable growth.

The increasing complexity of business operations necessitates a structured approach to project management, enabling organizations to navigate multifaceted challenges and optimize resource allocation. By employing systematic methodologies, businesses can ensure that projects are completed on time, within budget, and to the requisite quality standards. This systematic approach not only minimizes risks associated with project execution but also enhances the predictability of outcomes, thereby fostering stakeholder confidence.

Moreover, the globalization of markets has intensified the need for effective project management practices. Companies operating in diverse geographic locations must coordinate across time zones and cultural boundaries, necessitating robust communication and collaboration frameworks. Project management tools and techniques provide the necessary infrastructure to facilitate seamless interaction among distributed teams, enabling the integration of diverse perspectives and expertise. This global collaboration is pivotal in driving innovation and ensuring the delivery of products and services that meet the evolving demands of international consumers.

In addition to facilitating operational efficiency, project management plays a vital role in strategic planning and decision-making processes. By providing a structured framework for evaluating project feasibility and aligning initiatives with organizational goals, project management ensures that resources are allocated to projects that offer the greatest potential for value creation. This strategic alignment is critical in an environment where businesses must continuously adapt to changing market conditions and technological disruptions.

Furthermore, the role of project management extends beyond the confines of traditional industries. In sectors such as healthcare, education, and technology, project management principles are increasingly being applied to drive improvements in service delivery and operational performance. For instance, in the technology sector, agile project management methodologies have become synonymous with innovation, enabling rapid prototyping and iterative development cycles that respond swiftly to user feedback and market trends.

As organizations strive to enhance their sustainability credentials, project management is also becoming instrumental in implementing environmentally and socially responsible initiatives. By integrating sustainability considerations into project planning and execution, businesses can reduce their environmental footprint and contribute positively to societal well-being. This alignment with sustainable development goals not only enhances corporate reputation but also fosters long-term resilience in the face of evolving regulatory and consumer expectations.

In conclusion, project management is indispensable in modern business, underpinning the successful execution of strategic initiatives and fostering an environment conducive to innovation and growth. As businesses continue to navigate the complexities of the 21st-century landscape, the adoption of sophisticated project management practices will remain a critical determinant of organizational success. Through the effective deployment of project management tools and methodologies, businesses can unlock new avenues for value creation, ensuring their relevance and competitiveness in an ever-evolving global marketplace.

Key Concepts and Terminology

In the realm of project management, understanding key concepts and terminology is imperative for effective communication and execution of projects. This subchapter elucidates several foundational terms and concepts that are pivotal to navigating the intricacies of project management.

At the core of project management is the **project itself**, defined as a temporary endeavor undertaken to create a unique product, service, or result. Projects are characterized by their finite nature, typically having a defined beginning and end, and are often constrained by factors such as time, budget, and resources.

> **Scope** refers to the detailed set of deliverables or features of a project. The scope is fundamental in determining what is included in the project and what is not. Scope management ensures that the project includes all the work required to complete the project successfully, and nothing more.

Closely related is the concept of **scope creep**, which denotes the uncontrolled expansion of project scope without adjustments to time, cost, and resources. Effective scope management involves setting clear boundaries and maintaining strict oversight to prevent scope creep, which can derail a project.

Stakeholders are individuals or groups with an interest in the project's outcome. Identifying and managing stakeholders is crucial, as their influence can significantly affect the project's success. Stakeholder management involves understanding their expectations and requirements and ensuring they are met throughout the project lifecycle.

Project lifecycle is the series of phases that a project passes through from its initiation to its closure. Each phase is marked by a distinct set of tasks and objectives, and the lifecycle provides a structured approach to project execution. Common phases include initiation, planning, execution, monitoring and controlling, and closure.

Central to project management is the **triple constraint**, also known as the project management triangle, which refers to the balance of scope, time, and cost. These three constraints are interdependent; a change in one often affects the others. Effective project management seeks to optimize these constraints to achieve the desired outcome.

Risk management is a systematic process of identifying, analyzing, and responding to project risks. It involves risk identification, risk assessment, and the development of strategies to mitigate or capitalize on those risks. Proactive risk management is essential for minimizing the impact of uncertainties on the project.

Gantt charts and **PERT charts** are tools commonly used in project management for planning and scheduling. Gantt charts provide a visual timeline for the project, illustrating task durations and dependencies. PERT (Program Evaluation and Review Technique) charts focus on task sequencing and time estimates, helping project managers identify the critical path and potential bottlenecks.

Earned Value Management (EVM) is a project management technique used to measure project performance and progress. It integrates project scope, schedule, and cost to provide a comprehensive view of project health, enabling project managers to make informed decisions.

These key concepts and terminologies form the backbone of project management, providing a framework for understanding and executing projects effectively. Mastery of these elements is essential for any project manager seeking to deliver successful projects within the constraints of scope, time, and budget.

Chapter 2:

Initiating a Project

Understanding Project Scope

Project scope is a fundamental component in the discipline of project management, serving as the cornerstone upon which all subsequent planning and execution efforts are built. It encapsulates the entirety of work required to deliver a product, service, or result with specified features and functions. Understanding and defining the project scope is crucial as it sets the boundaries and establishes the parameters within which a project team operates.

The delineation of project scope begins with the development of a detailed project scope statement. This document is pivotal, outlining the project objectives, deliverables, and the criteria for success. It acts as a guiding document, ensuring that all stakeholders have a unified understanding of what the project intends to achieve and the constraints under which it will be executed.

A clear and precise project scope statement mitigates the risk of scope creep, a common challenge in project management where uncontrolled changes or continuous growth in a project's scope occur. Scope creep can lead to significant deviations from the original objectives, resulting in increased costs and extended timelines. Thus, it is imperative for project managers to establish a robust scope management plan, incorporating processes for scope verification and scope change control.

Critical to understanding project scope is the Work Breakdown Structure (WBS), a hierarchical decomposition of the total scope of work to be carried out by the project team. The WBS breaks down the project into smaller, more manageable components, facilitating better planning, execution, and control. Each level of the WBS represents a progressively detailed definition of the project work, ensuring that nothing is overlooked and that each element is accounted for.

Engaging stakeholders early in the scope definition process is essential. Stakeholders, including clients, team members, and other interested parties, provide valuable insights and requirements that shape the project scope. Their involvement ensures that the project outcomes align with their expectations and needs. Regular communication with stakeholders throughout the project lifecycle is vital to manage expectations and address any scope-related issues that may arise.

Establishing a well-defined project scope also involves identifying assumptions, constraints, and dependencies. Assumptions are factors considered to be true without empirical evidence, impacting the project's scope. Constraints are limitations or restrictions that the project must operate within, such as budgetary limits or regulatory requirements. Dependencies are relationships between tasks or deliverables that can influence the project timeline and scope.

In the context of project management, the scope is not static. It is subject to change due to evolving project conditions or stakeholder needs. Therefore, an effective scope management process includes mechanisms for evaluating potential changes and incorporating them into the project scope in a controlled manner. This involves assessing the impact of changes on the project's schedule, budget, and quality before deciding on their implementation.

Ultimately, understanding project scope is about achieving clarity and alignment among all project participants. It provides a framework for decision-making and prioritization, helping project teams stay focused on delivering value within the agreed-upon constraints. By mastering the intricacies of project scope, project managers are better equipped to lead their teams towards successful project completion.

Stakeholder Identification

The process of stakeholder identification is a fundamental component of effective project management. It involves the systematic identification and analysis of all parties who have a vested interest in the project, whether directly or indirectly. Stakeholders can significantly influence the project's success or failure, making their identification a critical step in the project planning phase.

A stakeholder can be defined as any individual, group, or organization that can affect or be affected by the project's outcomes. They can be internal or external to the organization and may include project sponsors, team members, customers, suppliers, regulatory bodies, and the community at large. Each stakeholder holds varying degrees of influence and interest in the project, necessitating a thoughtful and comprehensive approach to stakeholder identification.

The initial step in identifying stakeholders is to conduct a thorough stakeholder analysis. This process begins with the development of a stakeholder register, a document that lists all potential stakeholders along with relevant information such as their roles, interests, influence, and expectations. This register serves as a foundation for further analysis and engagement strategies.

To compile a comprehensive stakeholder register, project managers often employ various techniques. Brainstorming sessions with the project team can uncover potential stakeholders who may not be immediately apparent. Interviews and surveys with subject matter experts and organizational leaders can provide additional insights into stakeholders' roles and influence. Moreover, reviewing project documentation and organizational charts can help identify stakeholders who might otherwise be overlooked.

Once the stakeholders have been identified, they are analyzed in terms of their potential impact on the project. This involves assessing each stakeholder's level of interest and influence. Stakeholders with high influence and high interest are often prioritized, as their support or opposition can significantly affect the project's trajectory. Conversely, stakeholders with low interest and influence may require less attention but should still be monitored for any changes in their status.

A popular tool used for this analysis is the power/interest grid, which categorizes stakeholders based on their level of power and interest in the project. This visual representation aids project managers in determining the appropriate engagement strategies for each stakeholder group. For instance, stakeholders with high power and interest may necessitate regular communication and involvement in decision-making processes, while those with low power and interest may only require periodic updates.

Understanding the stakeholders' expectations and concerns is crucial for developing effective communication and engagement plans. This involves not only identifying their needs but also considering the potential conflicts that may arise between different stakeholder groups. Addressing these conflicts early in the project lifecycle helps in fostering a collaborative environment and securing stakeholder buy-in.

Stakeholder identification is not a one-time activity but an ongoing process throughout the project lifecycle. As projects evolve, new stakeholders may emerge, and existing ones may change their level of interest or influence. Continuous monitoring and reassessment of the stakeholder landscape ensure that the project remains aligned with stakeholder expectations and that potential risks are mitigated proactively.

In summary, stakeholder identification is a critical task in project management that requires careful analysis and strategic planning. By systematically identifying and understanding stakeholders, project managers can enhance communication, minimize conflicts, and increase the likelihood of project success. The effectiveness of this process is pivotal to the realization of project objectives and the satisfaction of all parties involved.

Setting Objectives and Goals

In the intricate domain of project management, the establishment of clear and measurable objectives and goals is paramount to the success of any project. This process serves as the cornerstone upon which the entire project framework is constructed, providing direction and a benchmark against which progress can be measured.

Objectives in project management are defined as specific outcomes that are to be achieved within a set timeframe. They are characterized by their precision and measurability, typically articulated through the SMART criteria—Specific, Measurable, Achievable, Relevant, and Time-bound. The specificity of objectives ensures that there is no ambiguity in what the project aims to achieve, while measurability allows for the quantification of progress, facilitating ongoing assessment and accountability.

Goals, on the other hand, are broader in nature, encapsulating the overall vision and end-result that the project seeks to accomplish. While objectives are often short-term and concrete, goals are more strategic and long-term, aligning closely with the overarching mission of the organization. The interplay between goals and objectives is crucial, as objectives serve as the stepping stones towards the realization of broader goals.

The process of setting objectives and goals begins with a comprehensive analysis of the project scope and stakeholder expectations. This involves engaging with key stakeholders to understand their needs, priorities, and constraints. Such engagement ensures that the objectives and goals are aligned with stakeholder expectations, enhancing the likelihood of project buy-in and support.

Once stakeholder insights are gathered, the next step involves the formulation of objectives and goals. This requires a collaborative approach, bringing together the project team, stakeholders, and subject matter experts to brainstorm and refine potential objectives. During this phase, it is essential to ensure that objectives are not only aligned with stakeholder needs but also achievable within the constraints of time, budget, and resources.

The articulation of objectives and goals must be documented in a clear and concise manner. This documentation serves as a reference point throughout the project lifecycle, guiding decision-making and prioritization. It is also essential for communicating the project's direction to all stakeholders, ensuring that everyone is on the same page.

Periodic review and adjustment of objectives and goals are necessary to accommodate changes in project scope or external factors. This dynamic approach ensures that the project remains aligned with its strategic goals, even as circumstances evolve. Such flexibility is crucial in today's rapidly changing business environment, where projects must often adapt to new challenges and opportunities.

In conclusion, the setting of objectives and goals is a critical component of effective project management. By providing a clear roadmap and criteria for success, they enable project managers to lead their teams with clarity and confidence. Moreover, well-defined objectives and goals facilitate the alignment of project activities with organizational strategy, ensuring that the project contributes to the broader mission and vision of the organization. Through careful planning, stakeholder engagement, and ongoing review, project managers can harness the power of objectives and goals to drive project success.

Project Charter Development

The project charter serves as the foundational document that formally authorizes a project and delineates the project's objectives, stakeholders, and deliverables. This pivotal document is a key artifact in project management, acting as a contract among stakeholders and providing a clear framework for the project's scope, resources, and timeline.

A well-constructed project charter begins with a succinct project title and description, which encapsulates the project's purpose and scope. This section should be precise yet comprehensive enough to convey the essence of the project to all stakeholders. The project objectives follow, outlining specific, measurable goals that the project seeks to achieve. These objectives should align with the organization's strategic goals, ensuring that the project contributes to broader business objectives.

Stakeholder identification is another critical element of the project charter. This involves recognizing all parties with vested interests in the project, ranging from project sponsors and team members to external partners and regulatory bodies. Understanding stakeholder needs and expectations is essential for fostering communication and collaboration throughout the project lifecycle.

The project charter also defines the project's scope, detailing the boundaries within which the project will operate. This includes identifying the primary deliverables and any constraints or limitations that might impact the project's execution. Clearly defining scope prevents scope creep, which can lead to project delays and cost overruns.

Resource allocation is addressed within the project charter, specifying the human, financial, and material resources required for successful project execution. This section should include an overview of the project budget and a preliminary timeline, highlighting major milestones and deadlines. Adequate resource planning ensures that the project is feasible and that sufficient support is available to achieve the project objectives.

Risk management is another integral component of the project charter. Identifying potential risks early in the project lifecycle allows for the development of mitigation strategies, thereby minimizing the impact of unforeseen events on project outcomes. The charter should outline a preliminary risk management plan, including the identification of high-level risks and proposed mitigation measures.

Roles and responsibilities within the project team are delineated in the project charter, establishing clear lines of authority and accountability. This section should specify the project manager's role, along with key team members' responsibilities, ensuring that everyone involved understands their contributions to the project's success.

The approval section of the project charter is where key stakeholders, including the project sponsor, formally endorse the document. This endorsement signifies commitment to the project and agreement to provide the necessary resources and support. The approval process ensures that all parties are aligned before project execution begins.

In essence, the project charter is more than just a formal document; it is a strategic tool that sets the stage for project success. By articulating clear objectives, defining scope, and establishing stakeholder commitments, the project charter provides a roadmap for navigating the complexities of project management. Its development requires a careful balance of detail and clarity, ensuring that all stakeholders have a shared understanding of the project's goals and the means by which they will be achieved.

Chapter 3:

Planning: Creating a Roadmap

Work Breakdown Structure

The Work Breakdown Structure (WBS) represents a cornerstone in the domain of project management, serving as a hierarchical decomposition of the total scope of work to be executed by the project team. It is an essential tool that provides a structured approach to organizing and defining the total work scope of the project, ensuring that all elements are accounted for and systematically arranged. This methodical breakdown facilitates meticulous planning, precise scheduling, and accurate cost estimation, thereby enhancing the efficiency and effectiveness of project execution.

The primary purpose of the WBS is to transform a complex project into manageable components, known as work packages, which can be independently planned, executed, and controlled. Each level of the WBS hierarchy delineates specific deliverables and project milestones, creating a clear pathway from the overarching project goals to the smallest actionable tasks. This hierarchical structure not only improves clarity and focus but also enables better communication among stakeholders, as each element is explicitly defined and understood in context.

At the top level of the WBS, the project is represented as a single entity, encapsulating the entire scope and objectives. This is subsequently divided into major deliverables or phases, which are further decomposed into smaller, more manageable components. Each subdivision represents a more detailed and specific aspect of the project, culminating in the work packages at the lowest level. These work packages are the fundamental building blocks of the WBS, detailing the tasks required to achieve the project objectives and enabling resource allocation, time estimation, and cost management.

The development of a WBS necessitates a comprehensive understanding of the project's scope and objectives. It requires collaboration among project stakeholders, including project managers, team members, and clients, to ensure that all aspects of the project are considered and integrated. This collaborative effort aids in identifying potential risks and dependencies, allowing for proactive risk management and contingency planning.

Furthermore, the WBS serves as a foundation for subsequent project management processes, including scheduling, budgeting, and resource allocation. By providing a clear and detailed outline of the project scope, it allows for the development of a realistic and achievable project plan. This plan serves as a roadmap for project execution, guiding the project team through each phase and ensuring that all deliverables are completed on time and within budget.

Moreover, the WBS is instrumental in facilitating project monitoring and control. By establishing clear performance metrics and milestones, it enables project managers to track progress, identify deviations from the plan, and implement corrective actions as needed. This ongoing monitoring ensures that the project remains aligned with its objectives and that any issues are addressed promptly to minimize impact.

In essence, the Work Breakdown Structure is a fundamental tool in project management, offering a structured and systematic approach to project planning and execution. Its ability to decompose complex projects into manageable components enhances clarity, communication, and control, ultimately contributing to the successful delivery of project objectives. As such, the WBS is an indispensable element in the toolkit of any project manager, providing a solid foundation for effective project management practices.

Resource Allocation

Effective resource allocation is a cornerstone of successful project management. It involves the strategic distribution and utilization of resources, including human capital, financial assets, time, and equipment, to achieve project objectives within defined constraints. The complexity of resource allocation arises from the need to balance competing demands and optimize the use of limited resources across multiple projects or tasks.

Central to the process of resource allocation is the identification of resource requirements, which involves assessing the needs of each project component. This assessment must consider the scope, scale, and timeline of the project, as well as the specific skills and expertise required. A thorough understanding of these factors allows project managers to allocate resources efficiently, ensuring that each task has the necessary support to be completed successfully.

A key principle in resource allocation is prioritization. Project managers must determine which tasks are most critical to the project's success and allocate resources accordingly. This often involves making difficult decisions about which projects or tasks will receive priority when resources are scarce. Prioritization can be guided by factors such as the strategic importance of a task, its impact on project timelines, and the potential risks associated with delays.

Resource leveling is another important aspect of resource allocation. This technique aims to minimize fluctuations in resource demand and ensure a consistent workload across the project lifecycle. By redistributing resources to balance workload, project managers can prevent bottlenecks and reduce the risk of burnout among team members. Effective resource leveling requires careful planning and continuous monitoring to adjust for changes in project scope or unexpected challenges.

In addition to balancing resource demands, project managers must also consider resource availability. This involves understanding the limitations of available resources and identifying potential constraints, such as budgetary restrictions or limited access to specialized equipment. By accounting for these constraints, project managers can develop realistic project plans that align with available resources.

Moreover, the dynamic nature of most projects necessitates flexibility in resource allocation. Project managers must be prepared to reallocate resources as project requirements change or as new information becomes available. This adaptability is crucial in responding to unforeseen challenges or opportunities that may arise during the project lifecycle.

To support effective resource allocation, many project managers utilize resource management tools and software. These tools provide valuable insights into resource utilization and availability, enabling project managers to make informed decisions about resource distribution. By leveraging technology, project managers can streamline the allocation process, improve accuracy, and enhance overall project efficiency.

Collaboration and communication also play a vital role in resource allocation. Project managers must work closely with team members, stakeholders, and other project managers to ensure that resources are allocated in a manner that aligns with project goals and organizational priorities. Open lines of communication facilitate the sharing of information and the identification of potential resource conflicts or synergies.

In summary, resource allocation is a complex but essential component of project management. It requires a strategic approach to balance resource demands, prioritize tasks, and adapt to changing project conditions. By mastering resource allocation, project managers can enhance project outcomes, optimize resource use, and contribute to the overall success of their organizations.

Risk Management Planning

Effective project management necessitates the foresight to anticipate potential pitfalls and the strategic acumen to mitigate these risks. At the heart of this proactive approach lies the discipline of risk management planning, a critical component that ensures project objectives are met with minimal disruptions. Risk management in project management is not merely a reactive measure but a systematic process that involves identifying, analyzing, and responding to risk factors throughout the lifecycle of a project.

The initial phase of risk management planning involves risk identification. This process requires a comprehensive understanding of both internal and external factors that could potentially impact the project. Techniques such as brainstorming sessions, expert interviews, and SWOT analysis are often employed to uncover potential risks. The identification process should encompass a wide range of risks, including technical challenges, financial constraints, regulatory compliance issues, and environmental factors.

Once risks have been identified, the next step is risk assessment. This involves evaluating the likelihood of each risk occurring and the potential impact on the project. Quantitative and qualitative methods are used for this assessment. Quantitative methods may include statistical models and simulations, while qualitative methods often involve risk matrices and scoring systems. The goal is to prioritize risks based on their potential impact and probability, allowing project managers to focus their efforts on the most significant threats.

Following assessment, risk response planning is crucial. This phase involves developing strategies to mitigate identified risks. The primary strategies include avoidance, mitigation, transfer, and acceptance. Avoidance involves altering the project plan to circumvent the risk entirely, while mitigation aims to reduce the impact or likelihood of the risk. Transfer shifts the risk to a third party, such as through insurance or outsourcing, whereas acceptance involves acknowledging the risk and preparing contingency plans.

Communication is a vital element of the risk management plan. Effective communication ensures that all stakeholders are aware of the potential risks and the strategies in place to manage them. Regular updates and transparent reporting are essential to maintain stakeholder confidence and ensure that everyone involved in the project is aligned with the risk management strategy.

Monitoring and controlling risks is an ongoing process throughout the project lifecycle. This involves tracking identified risks, reassessing their status, and identifying new risks as the project progresses. Regular risk audits and reviews should be conducted to ensure that risk management strategies remain effective and relevant. Adjustments may be necessary as new information becomes available or as the project evolves.

The integration of risk management planning into the overall project management process enhances the likelihood of project success. By systematically identifying, assessing, and managing risks, project managers can navigate uncertainties with greater confidence and agility. This proactive approach not only protects the project from potential setbacks but also fosters a culture of resilience and adaptability within the project team. In an ever-changing and complex project environment, robust risk management planning is indispensable, ensuring that projects are delivered on time, within budget, and to the satisfaction of all stakeholders.

Communication Plan

Effective communication is a cornerstone of successful project management. It involves the systematic dissemination and exchange of information between stakeholders to ensure alignment and facilitate the achievement of project objectives. A well-structured communication plan outlines the specific channels, methods, frequency, and responsibilities for information exchange, thus minimizing misunderstandings and enhancing collaboration.

The development of a communication plan begins with the identification of stakeholders and their information needs. Stakeholders may include project sponsors, team members, clients, vendors, and regulatory bodies, each with distinct perspectives and requirements. A thorough stakeholder analysis helps in tailoring communication strategies to address the unique priorities and concerns of each group.

Once stakeholders are identified, the next step involves defining the objectives of the communication plan. These objectives should align with the overall goals of the project and may include ensuring transparency, facilitating decision-making, and fostering stakeholder engagement. Clear objectives provide a framework for measuring the effectiveness of communication efforts and making necessary adjustments.

Choosing the appropriate communication channels is crucial for the effective transmission of information. Channels may range from formal methods such as reports and presentations to informal modes like emails and face-to-face meetings. The selection of channels depends on factors such as the complexity of the information, the urgency of the message, and the preferences of the stakeholders. A combination of synchronous and asynchronous communication methods can cater to diverse needs and schedules.

The frequency of communication is another critical element. Regular updates are essential to keep stakeholders informed of progress, challenges, and changes. The timing of these updates should be consistent with the project timeline and the decision-making cycles of stakeholders. For instance, weekly meetings may be appropriate for core team members, while monthly reports could suffice for executive stakeholders.

Assigning communication responsibilities ensures accountability and clarity in the dissemination of information. Roles may include a communication manager who oversees the plan's implementation, team leaders who provide updates on specific tasks, and a spokesperson who addresses media inquiries. Clearly defined roles prevent overlaps and gaps in communication, thereby enhancing efficiency.

Furthermore, the communication plan should incorporate feedback mechanisms to gauge stakeholder satisfaction and identify areas for improvement. Surveys, feedback forms, and informal check-ins can provide valuable insights into the effectiveness of communication strategies. This feedback loop enables continuous refinement of the plan to better meet stakeholder needs.

Risk management is an integral part of the communication plan. Proactive measures should be taken to address potential barriers such as language differences, technological failures, and cultural misunderstandings. Contingency plans should be in place to ensure uninterrupted communication in the face of unforeseen challenges.

Documentation of the communication plan is essential for transparency and accountability. A comprehensive document should outline the objectives, stakeholders, channels, frequency, responsibilities, and feedback mechanisms. This documentation serves as a reference for stakeholders and a guide for new team members.

In conclusion, a robust communication plan is instrumental in bridging the gap between diverse stakeholders and ensuring the smooth execution of project activities. By strategically planning and managing communication, project managers can foster a collaborative environment that drives project success.

Chapter 4:

Scheduling and Time Management

Estimating Time and Effort

Accurate estimation of time and effort is a fundamental skill in project management, crucial for planning, resource allocation, and meeting deadlines. This process involves predicting the total amount of time and effort required to complete a project or its components, often serving as the foundation for scheduling and budgeting decisions. Achieving precision in these estimates is challenging due to the inherent uncertainties and complexities of projects.

Factors Influencing Estimation

Several factors can influence the estimation process, including the project's scope, the experience of the project team, the availability of resources, and the complexity of tasks involved. The scope defines the breadth of the project, influencing the amount of work needed. A clear and detailed scope can aid in more accurate estimations. The experience level of the team also plays a critical role. Experienced team members can draw from past projects to make informed estimates, whereas less experienced teams may rely heavily on theoretical models.

Resource availability impacts the pace and efficiency with which tasks are completed. Limited or constrained resources can lead to longer timeframes and increased effort. Task complexity is another crucial factor; complex tasks with many dependencies or requiring specialized skills may demand more time and effort than simpler tasks.

Techniques for Estimation

Various techniques are employed to estimate time and effort, each with its strengths and limitations. **Analogous Estimation** relies on historical data from similar projects to predict future outcomes. This method is beneficial when historical data is relevant and readily available, allowing for quick and relatively accurate estimates. However, its accuracy diminishes when projects differ significantly from past experiences.

Parametric Estimation uses statistical models to predict project parameters based on historical data and other variables. This technique is effective when reliable data sets exist, providing more precise estimates by considering multiple factors influencing project outcomes. **Bottom-Up Estimation** involves breaking down the project into smaller, manageable components and estimating each part individually. This method can yield highly accurate results but is time-consuming and requires detailed project knowledge.

Three-Point Estimation introduces the concept of uncertainty into the estimation process by considering optimistic, pessimistic, and most likely scenarios. This approach helps in accounting for variability and provides a range of possible outcomes, enhancing the reliability of estimates.

Challenges and Mitigation Strategies

Despite the availability of various techniques, challenges in estimation persist. Cognitive biases, such as optimism bias, can lead to underestimating time and effort. To mitigate these, project managers can implement strategies such as engaging in rigorous stakeholder consultations, conducting peer reviews, and incorporating contingency buffers into estimates.

The dynamic nature of projects, characterized by changing requirements and unforeseen obstacles, also complicates estimation. Adopting an iterative approach, where estimates are continuously refined as more information becomes available, can help address this challenge. Additionally, leveraging project management software tools can facilitate data analysis and improve estimation accuracy.

Conclusion

Effective estimation of time and effort requires a blend of experience, analytical techniques, and adaptive strategies. By understanding the factors influencing estimation and employing appropriate techniques, project managers can enhance their ability to deliver projects on time and within budget, ultimately contributing to project success and organizational efficiency.

Developing a Project Schedule

The creation of a project schedule is a pivotal phase in project management, serving as the blueprint for the entire project lifecycle.

A well-structured schedule not only delineates the chronological sequence of tasks but also integrates resource allocation, cost estimation, and risk management. This subchapter delves into the essential methodologies and tools employed in developing an effective project schedule, highlighting the importance of precision and adaptability.

At the heart of schedule development is the Work Breakdown Structure (WBS), a hierarchical decomposition of the total scope of work to accomplish the project objectives. The WBS facilitates the identification of individual tasks, which are the fundamental units of the schedule. Each task is assigned a specific duration, and dependencies among tasks are established, ensuring a logical progression of activities. This step is crucial for maintaining the integrity of the project timeline.

To further refine the schedule, project managers employ techniques such as the Critical Path Method (CPM) and the Program Evaluation and Review Technique (PERT). CPM focuses on identifying the longest sequence of dependent tasks, known as the critical path, which determines the minimum project duration. PERT, on the other hand, introduces probabilistic time estimates, allowing for a more flexible approach to scheduling, particularly in projects with inherent uncertainties. These techniques are instrumental in identifying potential bottlenecks and optimizing task sequences to enhance efficiency.

Resource allocation is another critical aspect of schedule development. The assignment of personnel, equipment, and materials must align with the timeline to prevent resource shortages or surpluses. Resource leveling and resource smoothing are strategies employed to balance the demand for resources with their availability, ensuring that the schedule remains feasible and cost-effective. This requires continuous monitoring and adjustments, as resource constraints can significantly impact the project timeline.

Integrating risk management into the schedule is essential for anticipating and mitigating potential disruptions. Risk identification and analysis should be conducted at the outset, with contingency plans incorporated into the schedule to address unforeseen events. This proactive approach minimizes the impact of risks on the project timeline, enhancing the resilience of the schedule.

The use of project management software has revolutionized schedule development, offering sophisticated tools for planning, tracking, and analyzing project timelines. Software solutions provide visual representations of schedules through Gantt charts and network diagrams, facilitating communication and collaboration among project stakeholders. These tools also offer real-time updates, enabling project managers to respond swiftly to changes and maintain control over the project timeline.

Effective communication is paramount in schedule development, as it ensures that all stakeholders have a clear understanding of the project timeline and their respective roles. Regular meetings and progress reports foster transparency and accountability, allowing for timely identification and resolution of issues that may arise.

In conclusion, developing a project schedule is a complex yet vital component of project management. It requires a meticulous approach, integrating various methodologies and tools to construct a robust timeline that guides the project to successful completion. The dynamic nature of projects necessitates flexibility and continuous evaluation of the schedule to adapt to changes and challenges. By mastering the art of schedule development, project managers can steer their projects toward timely and efficient outcomes.

Critical Path Method

The Critical Path Method (CPM) is a pivotal technique in project management, which optimizes the scheduling of project activities. Developed in the late 1950s, CPM assists project managers in identifying the longest sequence of dependent tasks, known as the critical path, which determines the minimum project duration. By focusing on this path, project managers can allocate resources efficiently, manage time effectively, and anticipate potential delays.

At its core, CPM involves constructing a project model that includes a list of all activities required to complete the project, the time each activity will take, and the dependencies between these activities. This model is typically represented in a network diagram, where nodes symbolize activities and arrows indicate dependencies. The estimation of activity durations is crucial and often relies on historical data or expert judgment.

The process of identifying the critical path begins with a forward pass through the network diagram to calculate the earliest start (ES) and earliest finish (EF) times for each activity. This step ensures that all dependencies are respected and that each activity begins as soon as its predecessors are completed. Conversely, a backward pass is conducted to determine the latest start (LS) and latest finish (LF) times, ensuring that the project is completed by its deadline without any delay.

The critical path is characterized by activities where the total float, or slack, is zero. Float represents the amount of time an activity can be delayed without affecting the overall project completion date. Activities on the critical path have no room for delay, meaning any setback will directly impact the project's timeline. Therefore, monitoring these activities closely is essential for maintaining project schedules.

CPM is widely valued for its ability to highlight time-critical tasks and provide a clear timeline for project completion. It aids in identifying where project resources should be concentrated and facilitates effective communication among stakeholders. Additionally, CPM supports scenario analysis, allowing project managers to simulate various "what-if" scenarios to assess the potential impact of changes in activity durations or resource allocations.

Despite its advantages, CPM is not without limitations. The method assumes that activity durations are deterministic and does not account for the variability that can occur in real-world projects. Consequently, CPM is often used in conjunction with other techniques, such as Program Evaluation and Review Technique (PERT), which incorporates probabilistic time estimates.

In the realm of project management, CPM serves as a foundational tool for planning, scheduling, and controlling projects with precision. By leveraging this method, project managers can enhance their ability to deliver projects on time and within scope, thereby increasing the likelihood of project success. The critical path method remains a staple in the project manager's toolkit, providing a structured approach to navigating the complexities of project execution. It underscores the importance of strategic planning and the need for vigilance in tracking project progress, ensuring that projects are not only completed efficiently but also effectively meet stakeholder expectations.

As project management continues to evolve, CPM's principles endure, adapting to modern methodologies and technologies, reinforcing its relevance in contemporary project environments. This enduring utility highlights CPM's role as an indispensable strategy in the pursuit of mastering project management.

Time Management Tools and Techniques

Effective time management is a cornerstone of successful project management, facilitating the timely completion of tasks and ensuring that project objectives are met within established deadlines. This subchapter explores a range of tools and techniques that are instrumental in optimizing time management within the project management framework.

One of the primary methodologies employed in time management is the Work Breakdown Structure (WBS). This technique involves decomposing the project into smaller, manageable components. By breaking down the project into distinct tasks, project managers can allocate resources more effectively and establish a timeline that aligns with the project's overall objectives. The WBS serves as a foundational tool in identifying critical path activities and dependencies, which are crucial for developing a realistic project schedule.

The Gantt chart is another indispensable tool in the project manager's arsenal. This visual representation of a project schedule allows managers to track progress and identify potential bottlenecks. By illustrating start and end dates for each task, Gantt charts enable project managers to monitor the timeline continuously and make necessary adjustments to avoid delays. Moreover, Gantt charts facilitate communication among stakeholders by providing a clear overview of the project timeline.

Critical Path Method (CPM) is a technique used to identify the longest sequence of dependent tasks and determine the shortest time possible to complete the project. By focusing on the critical path, project managers can prioritize tasks that directly impact the project timeline, ensuring that resources are allocated efficiently to avoid delays. CPM is particularly useful in complex projects where multiple tasks are interdependent.

Program Evaluation and Review Technique (PERT) is another time management tool that assists in the planning and scheduling of projects. Unlike CPM, which uses a single time estimate, PERT employs three estimates: optimistic, pessimistic, and most likely. This probabilistic approach allows project managers to account for uncertainty and variability in task durations, providing a more flexible and realistic project schedule.

Resource leveling is a technique aimed at optimizing the allocation of resources to avoid over-allocation and ensure a balanced workload throughout the project lifecycle. By adjusting the start and end dates of tasks based on resource availability, project managers can prevent resource bottlenecks and ensure that all tasks are completed efficiently.

Time tracking software has become increasingly vital in modern project management. These digital tools enable project managers to monitor time spent on tasks in real-time, providing insights into productivity and allowing for adjustments in resource allocation. Time tracking software often integrates with other project management tools, offering comprehensive data that enhances decision-making processes.

Incorporating buffer times is a strategic approach to mitigating risks associated with unforeseen delays. By adding contingency time to the project schedule, managers can absorb the impact of unexpected events without compromising the overall timeline. This technique is particularly beneficial in projects with a high degree of uncertainty or complexity.

In the realm of project management, effective time management is not merely about adhering to schedules but also about optimizing processes to enhance productivity and prevent delays. By leveraging these tools and techniques, project managers can ensure that projects are completed on time, within budget, and to the satisfaction of stakeholders.

Chapter 5:

Budgeting and Cost Management

Estimating Costs

Effective cost estimation is a cornerstone of successful project management. It involves predicting the financial resources required to execute a project within its defined scope, schedule, and quality parameters. Accurate cost estimation ensures that a project is financially viable and provides a framework for financial control and decision-making throughout the project lifecycle.

Cost estimation begins with a comprehensive understanding of the project's scope and objectives. This understanding is achieved through detailed project planning and breakdown of work into manageable components. Each component is analyzed for its resource requirements, which include labor, materials, equipment, and overhead costs. These resources are then quantified and translated into monetary terms based on current market rates and historical data.

One of the primary methods used in cost estimation is the bottom-up approach. This method involves estimating the cost of each individual work package and aggregating these estimates to form the overall project cost. This approach is particularly useful for projects with well-defined tasks and activities, as it allows for detailed analysis and greater accuracy in cost prediction. However, it can be time-consuming and may require significant expertise and effort to ensure precision.

Alternatively, the top-down approach is employed for projects with less defined scopes or when time constraints limit detailed analysis. This method involves using historical data and expert judgment to estimate costs at a higher level, often based on analogous projects or industry standards. While quicker and less resource-intensive, this approach can be less accurate and may require adjustments as more detailed information becomes available.

Parametric estimating is another technique that leverages statistical relationships between historical data and project variables. This method uses mathematical models to predict costs based on key project parameters such as size, complexity, and duration. Parametric estimating is particularly effective when reliable data sets are available and can provide a quick and relatively accurate cost forecast.

In addition to these methods, cost estimation must also account for potential risks and uncertainties. Contingency allowances are incorporated to address unforeseen events or changes in project scope, which could impact costs. Sensitivity analysis and scenario planning are often employed to evaluate the impact of various risk factors on the project's financial performance.

The role of the project manager is critical in ensuring the accuracy and reliability of cost estimates. This involves not only selecting the appropriate estimation methods but also continuously monitoring and updating cost estimates as the project progresses. Regular cost reviews and variance analysis help identify potential cost overruns and enable timely corrective actions.

Moreover, effective communication of cost estimates to stakeholders is essential. Clear, transparent, and comprehensive cost reports foster stakeholder confidence and support informed decision-making. It is important that estimates are presented in a manner that is accessible and understandable to all project participants, ensuring alignment and commitment to the project's financial objectives.

In conclusion, cost estimation is an integral part of project management that requires a blend of analytical skills, historical insight, and strategic foresight. By employing a systematic approach to cost estimation, project managers can enhance financial predictability, optimize resource allocation, and ultimately contribute to the successful delivery of projects within budgetary constraints.

Budget Development

Effective budget development is a cornerstone of successful project management, necessitating a comprehensive understanding of the financial landscape within which a project operates. This process involves the meticulous estimation, allocation, and management of financial resources to ensure project objectives are met without exceeding available funds.

The first step in budget development is the precise estimation of costs associated with each aspect of the project. This involves identifying all tasks, resources, and potential contingencies that could impact the financial requirements of the project. Estimation techniques such as analogous estimating, parametric estimating, and bottom-up estimating are employed to derive realistic cost projections. Analogous estimating leverages historical data from similar projects to forecast costs, while parametric estimating uses statistical models to predict expenses based on project parameters. Bottom-up estimating, although more time-consuming, offers detailed insights by aggregating estimates for individual project components.

Once costs have been estimated, the next phase involves the strategic allocation of funds across various project activities. This requires a thorough understanding of project priorities and the identification of critical path activities that could significantly influence the project's timeline and success. Allocating resources effectively ensures that high-priority tasks receive adequate funding, while maintaining flexibility to address unforeseen challenges. This step also involves the establishment of financial baselines and benchmarks to monitor and control project expenditure.

Risk management plays a crucial role in budget development. Identifying potential risks and their financial implications allows project managers to set aside contingency reserves. These reserves act as financial buffers to mitigate the impact of unexpected events, ensuring that the project remains on track even in the face of adversity. Additionally, sensitivity analysis can be performed to assess the potential impact of various risk scenarios on the overall budget, allowing for more informed decision-making.

The integration of advanced project management software tools facilitates the budgeting process by providing real-time data analytics and financial modeling capabilities. These tools enable project managers to visualize budget allocations, track expenses, and generate financial reports with precision. The use of such technology enhances transparency and accountability, ensuring that project stakeholders are well-informed of the financial status throughout the project lifecycle.

Communication and collaboration among project stakeholders are vital to the success of budget development. Regular updates and open lines of communication help align financial expectations and foster a collective understanding of budgetary constraints. This collaborative approach encourages stakeholder buy-in and supports the identification of cost-saving opportunities through shared insights and expertise.

Ultimately, the success of budget development hinges on the ability to adapt and respond to changing project dynamics. Continuous monitoring of financial performance against established benchmarks allows for timely adjustments to be made, minimizing the risk of budget overruns. This iterative process, characterized by proactive management and strategic foresight, is essential for achieving project objectives within the defined financial parameters.

In conclusion, effective budget development is a dynamic and multifaceted process that requires a blend of analytical rigor, strategic planning, and collaborative engagement. By leveraging robust estimation techniques, risk management strategies, and advanced technological tools, project managers can navigate the complexities of financial planning to successfully deliver projects within budgetary constraints.

Cost Control Techniques

Effective cost control is a cornerstone of successful project management, demanding a systematic approach to monitoring and regulating expenditures within the constraints of a project budget. Managing costs requires a balance between planning, execution, and continuous assessment to ensure that a project remains financially viable.

At the core of cost control is the establishment of a comprehensive budget, which serves as a financial blueprint for the project. This budget is derived from detailed cost estimates, encompassing labor, materials, equipment, and any other resources necessary for project completion. To maintain financial control, project managers must employ various techniques that allow for real-time tracking and adjustment of project costs.

One fundamental technique is the implementation of a Work Breakdown Structure (WBS). The WBS dissects the project into smaller, manageable components, facilitating more precise cost estimation and allocation. By breaking down the project into distinct tasks or deliverables, project managers can assign specific budgets to each component, enhancing the granularity of financial oversight.

Another essential tool in cost control is Earned Value Management (EVM). EVM integrates project scope, schedule, and cost parameters, providing a holistic view of project performance. By comparing planned progress with actual accomplishments, EVM enables project managers to identify deviations from the budget early in the project lifecycle. Key metrics such as Cost Performance

Index (CPI) and Schedule Performance Index (SPI) are instrumental in assessing cost efficiency and schedule adherence.

Regular financial reporting is critical for maintaining transparency and accountability in project management. Cost reports should be generated at regular intervals, detailing expenditures against the planned budget. These reports serve as vital communication tools, informing stakeholders of the financial health of the project. Variance analysis, a component of these reports, is crucial for identifying discrepancies between budgeted and actual costs, allowing for timely corrective actions.

Change management is another vital aspect of cost control. Projects are dynamic, often subject to changes in scope or unforeseen challenges. A robust change management process ensures that any alterations to the project are evaluated for their financial implications before approval. This process involves documenting proposed changes, estimating their impact on project costs, and obtaining necessary approvals to integrate them into the project plan.

Resource leveling is a technique employed to optimize the allocation of resources, thereby minimizing costs associated with resource idleness or overutilization. By adjusting the project schedule or reassigning tasks, project managers can ensure that resources are used efficiently, reducing unnecessary expenditures.

Contingency planning is also integral to effective cost control. Allocating a contingency reserve within the budget provides a financial buffer for unforeseen expenses. This reserve acts as a safeguard, allowing the project to absorb unexpected costs without jeopardizing its financial stability.

The integration of technology in cost control has become increasingly prevalent, with project management software offering sophisticated tools for budget tracking and forecasting. These platforms provide real-time data analytics, enabling project managers to make informed financial decisions swiftly.

Ultimately, cost control is an ongoing process that requires vigilance and adaptability. By employing these techniques, project managers can ensure that projects are delivered within budget, thereby enhancing the likelihood of project success and stakeholder satisfaction.

Financial Reporting and Analysis

Financial reporting and analysis play a pivotal role in project management, serving as the cornerstone for informed decision-making and strategic planning. The discipline of financial reporting entails the systematic preparation and presentation of financial statements, providing a clear, factual representation of a project's financial status at given points in time. This process is essential for stakeholders, including project managers, investors, and regulatory bodies, to assess financial health, performance, and compliance.

The financial reports typically include the income statement, balance sheet, and cash flow statement. Each serves a unique purpose: the income statement reflects the project's profitability over a specific period; the balance sheet presents the financial position at a specific point in time, detailing assets, liabilities, and equity; and the cash flow statement provides insights into the cash inflows and outflows, crucial for assessing liquidity and financial flexibility.

In the realm of project management, these reports are not merely historical records. They are dynamic tools that guide strategic decisions. For instance, the analysis of financial ratios derived from these statements can reveal trends in profitability, efficiency, and liquidity, offering a quantitative basis for evaluating project performance. Ratios such as the current ratio, return on assets, and profit margins are indispensable for identifying potential financial issues before they escalate, thereby enabling proactive management.

Moreover, financial analysis extends beyond mere number-crunching; it involves a deep understanding of the project's context and the external economic environment. This comprehensive approach ensures that financial data is interpreted accurately, considering market trends, regulatory changes, and competitor actions. Such analysis is vital for risk management, allowing project managers to anticipate and mitigate financial risks that could jeopardize project success.

Budget variance analysis is another critical aspect of financial reporting in project management. By comparing actual financial performance against budgeted figures, project managers can pinpoint variances, investigate their causes, and implement corrective actions. This continuous monitoring and adjustment process helps maintain financial discipline, ensuring that projects remain on track both financially and operationally.

Furthermore, financial reporting and analysis facilitate transparency and accountability, building trust among stakeholders. Regular and accurate financial reporting ensures that all parties involved have a clear understanding of the project's financial trajectory, fostering an environment of openness and collaboration. This transparency is particularly crucial in large-scale projects involving multiple stakeholders, where financial mismanagement can lead to significant conflicts and setbacks.

In transitioning from financial reporting to strategic planning, the insights gleaned from financial analysis inform the allocation of resources, prioritization of tasks, and strategic direction. By aligning financial insights with project objectives, managers can make informed decisions that optimize resource utilization, enhance project outcomes, and ultimately drive project success.

Thus, financial reporting and analysis are not isolated tasks but integral components of a cohesive project management strategy. They provide the necessary financial intelligence that underpins effective planning, control, and execution, ensuring that projects not only meet their financial targets but also contribute to the broader organizational goals. Through meticulous financial reporting and insightful analysis, project managers can navigate the complexities of project finance, steering their projects toward successful completion and sustainable growth.

Chapter 6:

Quality Management in Projects

Defining Quality Standards

Quality standards in project management serve as a benchmark for evaluating the performance and outcome of a project. Establishing these standards is a crucial step in ensuring that the deliverables meet the expectations of stakeholders and comply with regulatory requirements. The process begins with a comprehensive understanding of the project scope and the specific needs of the client or end-user.

At the core of defining quality standards is the identification of key performance indicators (KPIs) that align with the project's objectives. These indicators provide measurable metrics that can be monitored throughout the project lifecycle, offering a clear framework for assessing progress and quality. It is essential to engage stakeholders in this process to ensure that the KPIs reflect their priorities and expectations.

The development of quality standards also involves the establishment of quality control processes. These processes include routine inspections, testing, and validation procedures that are integrated into the project timeline. By implementing these controls, project managers can detect and address potential issues early, minimizing the risk of defects and rework.

Moreover, quality assurance practices play a vital role in maintaining the integrity of the project. These practices involve systematic activities and procedures that ensure the project will satisfy the relevant quality standards. Quality assurance is proactive, focusing on preventing defects through planned and systematic activities. This contrasts with quality control, which is reactive, identifying defects after they occur.

Another critical aspect of defining quality standards is the documentation of procedures and guidelines. This documentation serves as a reference for project teams, outlining the accepted methods and practices that should be followed. It also provides a basis for training new team members and promoting consistency across the project.

In addition to internal standards, project managers must consider external standards and regulations that may impact the project. These can include industry-specific standards, environmental regulations, and safety requirements. Adherence to these standards is not only a matter of compliance but also enhances the credibility and reputation of the project and the organization.

The involvement of the project team is crucial in the development and implementation of quality standards. By fostering a culture of quality, team members are encouraged to take ownership of their work and continuously seek improvements. Regular training sessions and workshops can help reinforce the importance of quality and equip team members with the necessary skills and knowledge.

Finally, the role of technology in defining and maintaining quality standards cannot be overlooked. Tools such as project management software, automated testing systems, and data analytics platforms provide valuable support in monitoring quality metrics and identifying areas for improvement. These technologies enable more efficient and accurate tracking of project performance, facilitating timely decision-making and corrective actions.

In summary, defining quality standards is a multifaceted process that requires careful planning and collaboration. By establishing clear benchmarks and integrating quality control and assurance practices, project managers can enhance the likelihood of project success and deliver outcomes that meet or exceed stakeholder expectations. By doing so, they not only ensure the project's success but also contribute to the ongoing development and improvement of project management practices.

Quality Assurance Processes

Quality assurance (QA) processes serve as a cornerstone in the realm of project management, ensuring that the deliverables meet predefined standards and satisfy client expectations. The establishment of a rigorous QA framework is vital to mitigate risks, enhance product reliability, and foster client trust. This subchapter delves into the essential components and methodologies of quality assurance processes, providing a comprehensive understanding of their application within project management.

At the heart of QA processes lies the development of a quality management plan, which articulates the quality objectives, metrics, and activities necessary for achieving the desired level of quality. This plan acts as a roadmap, guiding the project team through various quality assurance activities. It delineates the roles and responsibilities of team members, sets forth the standards and regulations to be adhered to, and outlines the tools and techniques for quality assessment.

One of the fundamental methodologies employed in QA is statistical process control (SPC), which involves the use of statistical methods to monitor and control quality. SPC aids in identifying variations in processes, enabling timely corrective actions to prevent defects and ensure consistency. By implementing control charts, project managers can visualize process performance over time, facilitating the detection of trends and anomalies that may compromise quality.

Another pivotal element of QA is the conduct of audits and reviews. These systematic examinations provide an objective evaluation of the project's adherence to quality standards. Audits may be internal or external, each serving to verify compliance with established procedures and identify areas for improvement. Regular reviews, such as peer reviews or management reviews, foster transparency and accountability, ensuring that quality remains a priority throughout the project lifecycle.

The integration of quality assurance with risk management is also crucial. QA processes must be aligned with risk management strategies to proactively identify potential quality issues and address them before they escalate. By conducting risk assessments and implementing mitigation plans, project managers can reduce the likelihood of quality-related setbacks and enhance overall project resilience.

Furthermore, continuous improvement is a key tenet of quality assurance. By embracing a culture of continuous improvement, organizations can refine their processes, adapt to changing requirements, and maintain competitiveness. Tools such as Six Sigma and Lean methodologies offer structured approaches to process improvement, emphasizing the elimination of waste and the pursuit of excellence.

Training and development of project personnel play a significant role in the effective implementation of QA processes. Ensuring that team members possess the requisite skills and knowledge is essential for maintaining high-quality standards. Regular training sessions, workshops, and seminars can equip the team with the latest industry practices and technological advancements, fostering a culture of quality consciousness.

In conclusion, quality assurance processes are integral to the successful execution of projects. By establishing a robust QA framework, employing statistical and audit methodologies, integrating with risk management, and promoting continuous improvement, project managers can safeguard quality and deliver superior outcomes. The commitment to quality not only enhances project performance but also fortifies client relationships, paving the way for sustained success in the competitive landscape of project management.

Quality Control Techniques

Quality control is an essential aspect of project management that ensures the final deliverable meets the predefined standards and requirements. In the realm of project management, various quality control techniques are employed to monitor and maintain the quality of processes and outputs. These techniques not only help in identifying defects but also in taking corrective actions to prevent future occurrences.

Statistical process control (SPC) is a fundamental technique used to monitor and control a process through statistical methods. It involves the use of control charts to track the performance of a process over time. By analyzing data points and identifying patterns, project managers can detect variations that may indicate potential problems. This proactive approach allows for timely interventions, thus maintaining process consistency and product quality.

Another widely used technique is the Pareto analysis, which is based on the Pareto Principle, also known as the 80/20 rule. This technique helps in identifying the most significant factors in a process that contribute to the majority of problems. By focusing on these key areas, project managers can prioritize their efforts and resources to achieve the greatest impact on quality improvement.

The use of cause-and-effect diagrams, commonly known as fishbone diagrams or Ishikawa diagrams, provides a visual representation of the potential causes of a problem. This technique facilitates brainstorming sessions, enabling project teams to systematically explore and identify root causes of defects. By addressing these root causes, project managers can implement effective solutions to enhance quality.

Check sheets are a simple yet powerful tool for collecting and analyzing data. They provide a structured format for recording and categorizing information, making it easier to identify patterns and trends. This technique is particularly useful in the early stages of quality control, where data collection is critical for informed decision-making.

Histograms are graphical representations of data distribution and are instrumental in understanding the frequency and variation of data points. By visualizing data in this manner, project managers can quickly identify deviations from expected performance, thus enabling corrective actions to be taken promptly.

Control charts, as part of SPC, are used to determine whether a process is stable and predictable. These charts plot data points over time and include control limits that define the boundaries of acceptable variation. By monitoring these charts, project managers can identify trends, shifts, or outliers that may indicate process instability.

Scatter diagrams, another useful tool, help in identifying relationships between two variables. By plotting data on a graph, project managers can ascertain whether changes in one variable correlate with changes in another. This analysis is crucial for identifying causal relationships and implementing strategies to enhance quality.

Quality control techniques also involve the use of inspection and testing to verify that products or services meet the required specifications. Regular inspections ensure that any defects are identified and rectified before the final delivery. Testing, on the other hand, involves evaluating a product's performance under specified conditions to ensure its compliance with quality standards.

Incorporating these quality control techniques into project management practices not only ensures the achievement of quality objectives but also fosters a culture of continuous improvement. By systematically applying these methods, project managers can enhance efficiency, reduce costs, and deliver products and services that meet or exceed stakeholder expectations.

Continuous Improvement

Continuous improvement is an integral aspect of project management that seeks to optimize processes, enhance productivity, and ensure quality outcomes. It involves the systematic identification and elimination of inefficiencies through incremental enhancements and innovations. The concept is rooted in the philosophy of Kaizen, which translates to "change for better" and emphasizes that small, ongoing positive changes can yield significant improvements over time.

In the realm of project management, continuous improvement is not merely an optional practice but a necessity to remain competitive and relevant. It demands a structured approach to reviewing and refining project processes. This often involves leveraging feedback loops, conducting retrospectives, and utilizing performance metrics to guide decision-making.

A fundamental aspect of continuous improvement is the Plan-Do-Check-Act (PDCA) cycle, initially developed by W. Edwards Deming. This iterative loop serves as a framework for problem-solving and process enhancement. In the planning phase, objectives are established, and strategies to achieve these goals are formulated. The subsequent "Do" phase involves the implementation of these strategies. During the "Check" phase, outcomes are evaluated against the set objectives, identifying any deviations or areas for further improvement. Finally, the "Act" phase involves making the necessary adjustments to rectify issues and enhance processes.

The success of continuous improvement initiatives hinges on cultivating a culture that encourages experimentation and learning. Project teams should be empowered to explore innovative solutions and learn from both successes and failures. This requires fostering an environment where open communication and collaboration are prioritized, allowing team members to share insights and propose improvements without fear of repercussion.

Another critical component of continuous improvement is leveraging technology and data analytics. With the advent of advanced project management tools, teams can gain valuable insights into project performance and identify trends or patterns that may indicate inefficiencies. These technologies enable real-time monitoring and facilitate data-driven decision-making, ensuring that improvement efforts are targeted and effective.

Moreover, continuous improvement should be aligned with organizational objectives and stakeholder expectations. This alignment ensures that efforts are not only focused on enhancing project-specific processes but also contribute to broader business goals. Regular engagement with stakeholders provides valuable insights into their evolving needs and expectations, allowing project managers to tailor improvement initiatives accordingly.

Training and development play a pivotal role in equipping project teams with the skills and knowledge required to drive continuous improvement. Regular workshops, seminars, and knowledge-sharing sessions can help teams stay abreast of the latest methodologies and tools in project management. Furthermore, recognizing and rewarding contributions to improvement initiatives can motivate team members to actively participate in the process.

Incorporating continuous improvement into project management practices results in numerous benefits, including increased efficiency, reduced costs, and enhanced customer satisfaction. By adopting a proactive approach to identifying and addressing inefficiencies, organizations can achieve sustainable growth and maintain a competitive edge in their respective industries. The journey of continuous improvement is ongoing, requiring commitment and adaptability as project landscapes evolve. By embedding this philosophy into the core of project management practices, organizations can ensure long-term success and resilience in an ever-changing environment.

Chapter 7:

Human Resource Management

Building a Project Team

The foundation of any successful project lies in the deliberate assembly of a project team, a task that requires meticulous attention to both the technical and interpersonal dynamics of potential team members. Project management, as a discipline, necessitates a strategic approach to team composition, ensuring that the collective capabilities align with the project's objectives and scope.

Central to this process is the identification and selection of individuals who possess not only the requisite technical expertise but also the capacity for collaboration and adaptability in dynamic environments. The project manager must evaluate potential team members on multiple dimensions: technical skills, problem-solving abilities, communication proficiency, and the potential for contributing to a cohesive team dynamic. This evaluation often involves a rigorous assessment of past performance, technical certifications, and interviews to ascertain alignment with the project's goals.

Once potential team members are identified, the project manager must consider the optimal configuration of the team. This involves assigning roles and responsibilities that leverage each member's strengths while fostering a sense of ownership and accountability. The role allocation process is critical, as it directly influences the team's efficiency and effectiveness. A well-structured team not only meets technical demands but also navigates interpersonal challenges with agility, ensuring that conflicts are resolved constructively and that diverse perspectives are harnessed to enhance problem-solving.

The project manager must also establish a framework for communication and collaboration that supports the team's objectives. This framework should include regular meetings, clear channels for information dissemination, and tools that facilitate both synchronous and asynchronous communication. Effective communication is the linchpin of team cohesion, enabling members to share insights, address challenges, and make informed decisions collaboratively. The use of collaborative technologies, such as project management software and communication platforms, is essential in maintaining transparency and enabling real-time decision-making.

The dynamics of a project team are further influenced by the organizational culture and the external environment. The project manager must navigate these influences, ensuring that the team operates within the organization's strategic framework while adapting to external pressures and stakeholder expectations. This requires a nuanced understanding of organizational behavior and the ability to mediate between the project team's needs and the broader organizational objectives.

Moreover, the project manager should foster a culture of continuous improvement within the team. This involves encouraging feedback, recognizing achievements, and facilitating professional development opportunities. By promoting an environment where team members can enhance their skills and knowledge, the project manager not only strengthens the team's capabilities but also enhances individual motivation and commitment to the project's success.

Ultimately, the construction of a project team is a dynamic process that requires ongoing evaluation and adaptation. The project manager must remain vigilant, monitoring team performance and making adjustments as necessary to address emerging challenges and opportunities. Through strategic planning, effective communication, and adaptive leadership, the project manager can build a project team that is not only capable of achieving the project's objectives but also resilient in the face of unforeseen challenges.

Roles and Responsibilities

In the realm of project management, the delineation of roles and responsibilities is paramount to the successful execution of any project. This subchapter delves into the intricacies of defining and assigning roles within a project team, emphasizing the importance of clarity and structure in achieving project objectives.

A project manager's role is multifaceted, requiring a blend of leadership, communication, and organizational skills. The project manager acts as the linchpin, coordinating between various stakeholders, ensuring that the project adheres to its timeline, budget, and scope. This individual is responsible for setting the tone of the project, fostering a collaborative environment, and resolving conflicts that may arise.

Below the project manager, the project team comprises individuals with specialized skills tailored to the project's needs. Each team member must understand their specific responsibilities and how their contributions align with the project's goals. This alignment is crucial for maintaining motivation and ensuring efficient workflow.

The project sponsor plays a critical role, providing the necessary resources and support to the project manager and team. The sponsor's involvement is crucial for securing organizational buy-in and ensuring that the project aligns with the broader strategic objectives of the organization. The sponsor must maintain a balance between oversight and empowerment, allowing the project manager the autonomy to make decisions while providing guidance and support as needed.

Stakeholders, both internal and external, are integral to the project's success. They possess vested interests in the project's outcomes and can influence project direction. Effective stakeholder management involves identifying key stakeholders, understanding their expectations, and engaging them appropriately throughout the project lifecycle. Regular communication and feedback mechanisms are essential to align stakeholder expectations with project deliverables.

The roles of team members are often defined by their expertise and the specific requirements of the project. Technical experts provide the necessary skills and knowledge to tackle complex problems, while support roles such as administrative and financial personnel ensure that logistical aspects are managed efficiently. Each role, though distinct, contributes to a cohesive effort towards project completion.

Clear role definitions and responsibilities help in avoiding overlaps and gaps in accountability. It is essential for the project manager to establish a responsibility assignment matrix, often referred to as a RACI chart (Responsible, Accountable, Consulted, Informed), to document who is responsible for each task, who is accountable for outcomes, who needs to be consulted, and who should be kept informed. This tool is invaluable for ensuring transparency and accountability within the team.

Effective communication is the cornerstone of successful role execution. Regular meetings, status updates, and open channels of communication facilitate the exchange of information and help in preemptively addressing potential issues. The project manager must ensure that all team members are informed and engaged, fostering a culture of inclusivity and shared responsibility.

In conclusion, well-defined roles and responsibilities are integral to the success of a project. By establishing clear expectations and fostering open communication, project managers can create an environment where each team member understands their contribution to the project's success. This clarity not only enhances efficiency but also mitigates risks, paving the way for successful project delivery.

Team Development

Effective team development is a cornerstone of successful project management. This subchapter delves into the intricacies of forming, nurturing, and maintaining high-performance teams within the context of project management.

The process of team development can be conceptualized through Tuckman's stages: forming, storming, norming, and performing. Each stage presents unique challenges and opportunities that project managers must navigate to optimize team dynamics.

Forming Stage

In the initial forming stage, team members are introduced and start to understand the project's scope and objectives. During this phase, roles and responsibilities are typically defined, and the team begins to establish ground rules and processes. The project manager plays a crucial role in facilitating introductions and encouraging open communication to help build trust among team members. A clear articulation of project goals and individual roles is essential to set the foundation for effective collaboration.

Storming Stage

As the team progresses to the storming stage, conflicts may arise as individuals assert their ideas and perspectives. This phase is characterized by power struggles and competition, which can potentially derail project progress if not managed effectively. The project manager must employ conflict resolution strategies, such as active listening and mediation, to guide the team through this turbulent period. Encouraging a culture of respect and open dialogue can help mitigate the negative impacts of this stage.

Norming Stage

The norming stage marks the transition from individualism to a more cohesive group dynamic. Team members begin to appreciate each other's strengths and work collaboratively towards common goals. The project manager should focus on reinforcing team norms, encouraging cooperation, and recognizing achievements. Establishing regular feedback loops and celebrating small victories can enhance team morale and foster a sense of collective ownership over the project outcomes.

Performing Stage

In the performing stage, the team reaches a level of maturity where it operates efficiently and effectively towards project objectives. Team members are highly motivated, and their interactions are characterized by trust and mutual respect. The project manager's role evolves into that of a facilitator, providing support and resources as needed while empowering team members to take initiative and make decisions. Continuous improvement practices should be encouraged to maintain high performance levels.

Team Development Strategies

To support these stages of development, project managers can employ various strategies. Regular team-building activities can strengthen interpersonal relationships and improve communication. Training programs that focus on skills development and knowledge sharing can enhance individual and team capabilities. Additionally, fostering an inclusive environment where diversity of thought is valued can lead to innovative solutions and improved problem-solving.

Challenges and Considerations

Despite best efforts, team development is not without its challenges. Cultural differences, varying work styles, and remote working arrangements can impede team cohesion. Project managers must be adept at recognizing and addressing these challenges through adaptive leadership and tailored interventions. Emphasizing transparency and accountability within the team can help overcome barriers and maintain alignment with project goals.

In conclusion, effective team development is integral to the success of project management endeavors. By understanding and skillfully navigating the stages of team development, project managers can cultivate high-performing teams that drive project success. The ability to foster collaboration, resolve conflicts, and inspire motivation is paramount in building teams that not only achieve but exceed project objectives.

Conflict Resolution

Conflict is an inevitable aspect of project management, arising from diverse stakeholder interests, resource constraints, and ambiguous objectives. Understanding and effectively managing conflicts are critical skills for project managers, as unresolved disputes can lead to project delays, cost overruns, and diminished team morale.

This subchapter delves into the nature of conflicts within project environments and explores methodologies for resolving them in a constructive manner.

Conflicts in project management are typically categorized into three primary types: task-related, process-oriented, and interpersonal. Task-related conflicts stem from disagreements over project goals, priorities, or the allocation of resources. Process-oriented conflicts arise from differences in opinions regarding the methodologies or strategies employed to achieve project objectives. Interpersonal conflicts, on the other hand, emerge from personality clashes, communication breakdowns, or cultural differences among team members.

The first step in conflict resolution is identifying the underlying causes and understanding the perspectives of all parties involved. Open and empathetic communication is essential in this phase, as it allows project managers to gather comprehensive insights into the root causes of the conflict. Active listening and asking probing questions can help reveal hidden concerns and facilitate a deeper understanding of the issues at hand.

Once the causes of the conflict are identified, project managers can employ various conflict resolution strategies. One common approach is negotiation, which involves collaborative discussions aimed at reaching a mutually acceptable solution. Effective negotiation requires a willingness to compromise and a focus on finding win-win outcomes that satisfy all parties involved. This approach not only resolves the immediate conflict but also strengthens relationships and fosters a collaborative team environment.

Another strategy is mediation, where a neutral third party facilitates discussions between conflicting parties. The mediator guides the dialogue, ensuring that each party has an opportunity to express their views and work towards a resolution. Mediation can be particularly effective in complex conflicts involving multiple stakeholders, as it provides a structured framework for dialogue and problem-solving.

In some cases, conflicts may require arbitration, where an independent arbitrator makes a binding decision to resolve the dispute. While arbitration is less collaborative than negotiation or mediation, it can be a necessary measure when parties are unable to reach an agreement through other means. It is important for project managers to weigh the potential impacts of arbitration on team dynamics and project outcomes before proceeding with this approach.

Preventive measures can also play a significant role in minimizing conflicts. Establishing clear communication channels, setting well-defined project goals, and fostering a culture of transparency and trust are essential for preventing misunderstandings and reducing the likelihood of conflicts arising. Regular team meetings, feedback sessions, and conflict management training can further equip team members with the skills needed to handle disputes constructively.

Ultimately, the ability to navigate and resolve conflicts is a hallmark of effective project management. By employing a combination of communication, negotiation, and mediation techniques, project managers can transform potential obstacles into opportunities for growth and innovation, thereby enhancing team cohesion and ensuring project success. Understanding the dynamics of conflict and mastering resolution strategies are indispensable components of a project manager's skill set, essential for steering projects towards successful completion.

Chapter 8:

Effective Communication

Communication Models and Theories

Effective communication is the cornerstone of successful project management. Understanding the underlying models and theories that govern communication processes is essential for project managers aiming to navigate complex interactions within teams and across organizational boundaries. This subchapter delves into the foundational communication models and theories, offering insights into their application within the project management context.

Linear Model of Communication

The linear model, often considered the simplest form of communication, posits a one-way transmission of information from a sender to a receiver. This model emphasizes clarity and precision in message delivery, ensuring that the intended message is transmitted without distortion. In project management, this model is particularly relevant during the dissemination of project objectives, timelines, and deliverables, where unidirectional communication is often sufficient to convey critical information.

Interactive Model of Communication

Building upon the linear model, the interactive model introduces the concept of feedback, recognizing communication as a two-way process. Feedback loops allow for clarification and adjustment of messages, reducing the likelihood of misunderstandings. In project environments, interactive communication is pivotal during stakeholder meetings and team discussions, where feedback ensures alignment and fosters collaborative decision-making.

Transactional Model of Communication

The transactional model further refines the communication process by acknowledging the simultaneous sending and receiving of messages by all parties involved. It highlights the dynamic and continuous nature of communication, where context, relationships, and social systems influence the exchange of information. For project managers, this model underscores the importance of context awareness and adaptability, allowing them to respond to nuances in team dynamics and external stakeholder interactions.

Shannon-Weaver Model

The Shannon-Weaver model introduces the concept of noise, recognizing that communication can be hindered by various forms of interference. In project management, noise may manifest as technical jargon, cultural differences, or organizational barriers. Understanding this model helps project managers identify potential sources of noise and implement strategies to mitigate their impact, such as simplifying technical language or fostering an inclusive communication environment.

Schramm's Model of Communication

Schramm's model emphasizes the role of shared experiences in effective communication. It posits that communication is most successful when the sender and receiver share common fields of experience. In project management, this model highlights the importance of establishing a common knowledge base among team members and stakeholders, facilitating more meaningful and efficient exchanges.

Berlo's SMCR Model

Berlo's Source-Message-Channel-Receiver (SMCR) model focuses on the components of communication, stressing the importance of the source's credibility, the clarity of the message, the appropriateness of the channel, and the receiver's ability to comprehend the message. Project managers can apply this model by carefully selecting communication channels and tailoring messages to suit their audience, ensuring that information is effectively conveyed and understood.

Incorporating these communication models and theories into project management practices enhances the ability to convey information accurately, foster collaboration, and navigate the complexities of stakeholder interactions. By understanding and applying these models, project managers can optimize communication strategies, ultimately leading to more successful project outcomes.

Tools for Effective Communication

Effective communication is the bedrock upon which successful project management is built. It involves the seamless exchange of information and ideas, ensuring that all stakeholders are aligned and informed. To achieve this, project managers must employ a range of tools that facilitate clear, concise, and efficient communication across various platforms and formats.

One of the primary tools utilized in project management is email communication. While seemingly basic, the strategic use of emails can significantly enhance the flow of information. Emails allow for the documentation of conversations, the dissemination of important updates, and the provision of a reference point for future discussions. Project managers should adopt best practices such as using clear subject lines, bullet points for key information, and ensuring that emails are targeted to the relevant stakeholders.

Meetings, whether virtual or face-to-face, are another critical communication tool. They provide a forum for real-time discussion, problem-solving, and decision-making. To maximize their effectiveness, meetings should be well-structured with a clear agenda, defined objectives, and a set time limit. The use of video conferencing tools, such as Zoom or Microsoft Teams, has become increasingly prevalent, allowing for the inclusion of remote team members and fostering a sense of collaboration regardless of geographical boundaries.

Project management software tools, such as Asana, Trello, or Microsoft Project, play a pivotal role in facilitating communication. These platforms offer a centralized space for task management, deadline tracking, and progress updates. They enable team members to communicate asynchronously, reducing the need for constant meetings and allowing for more flexible working arrangements. Additionally, these tools often integrate with other communication platforms, streamlining the flow of information.

Instant messaging platforms, such as Slack or Microsoft Teams, cater to the need for quick, informal communication. They allow team members to engage in real-time conversations, share files, and collaborate on tasks without the formality of emails or the need to schedule meetings. This immediacy helps in addressing urgent issues swiftly and maintaining a steady momentum in project progress.

Visual communication tools, such as PowerPoint and Canva, are essential for presenting complex information in an easily digestible format. Diagrams, charts, and infographics can convey data-driven insights more effectively than text alone, aiding in the understanding and retention of information. These tools are particularly useful during presentations, stakeholder briefings, and team meetings.

Feedback mechanisms, such as surveys or feedback forms, are crucial for assessing the effectiveness of communication strategies and tools. They provide valuable insights into stakeholder perceptions and areas for improvement. Regularly soliciting feedback ensures that communication remains aligned with the needs and preferences of the team and stakeholders.

Incorporating a blend of these tools into a cohesive communication strategy enables project managers to navigate the complexities of project management effectively. By fostering an environment of transparency, collaboration, and responsiveness, these tools help in mitigating misunderstandings, enhancing productivity, and ultimately driving project success. Effective communication is not merely about the transmission of information; it is about building relationships, fostering trust, and ensuring that the project vision is realized through collective effort and shared understanding.

Managing Stakeholder Expectations

Project management is inherently a multifaceted discipline, necessitating a strategic and systematic approach to managing various elements, including stakeholder expectations. Stakeholders, encompassing individuals, groups, or organizations that have an interest in the project's outcome, play a pivotal role in its success or failure. Thus, managing their expectations is not only crucial but a determinant factor in ensuring project alignment and achieving desired outcomes.

The complexity of managing stakeholder expectations arises from their diverse perspectives, interests, and levels of influence. Stakeholders may include project sponsors, team members, end-users, regulatory bodies, and even the community at large. Each group brings its own set of expectations, which can often be conflicting. Therefore, it is imperative for project managers to employ a structured approach to effectively address these expectations.

A fundamental component of managing stakeholder expectations is the identification and analysis of stakeholders. This involves a thorough examination of who the stakeholders are, their interests, influence, and potential impact on the project. Tools such as stakeholder mapping and analysis matrices can be employed to systematically categorize stakeholders based on their power and interest levels. This categorization aids in prioritizing stakeholders and tailoring communication strategies accordingly.

Once stakeholders are identified and analyzed, clear communication becomes paramount. Effective communication is a cornerstone in managing expectations, as it facilitates transparency and fosters trust. Establishing a robust communication plan that outlines the frequency, medium, and content of interactions with stakeholders is essential. This plan should be adaptable to accommodate changes in stakeholder needs and project dynamics.

Furthermore, setting realistic and attainable expectations from the onset is crucial. This involves aligning stakeholders' expectations with the project's objectives, scope, and constraints. It is essential to engage stakeholders in the project planning phase, ensuring that their inputs are considered and that they have a clear understanding of what the project aims to achieve. By doing so, project managers can mitigate risks associated with unrealistic expectations that could lead to dissatisfaction or project derailment.

Continuous engagement with stakeholders throughout the project lifecycle is another critical element in managing expectations. Regular updates, feedback sessions, and review meetings provide opportunities to address concerns, clarify misunderstandings, and reinforce stakeholder buy-in. This ongoing engagement ensures that stakeholders remain informed and engaged, reducing the likelihood of misaligned expectations.

Lastly, it is vital to manage changes in stakeholder expectations as the project progresses. Change is inevitable, and stakeholders may refine their expectations based on evolving project conditions. A well-defined change management process that includes stakeholder involvement ensures that modifications are systematically evaluated and communicated, minimizing disruptions and maintaining project alignment.

In sum, managing stakeholder expectations is a dynamic and ongoing process that requires a blend of strategic planning, clear communication, and adaptive management. By effectively managing these expectations, project managers can enhance stakeholder satisfaction, foster collaborative relationships, and ultimately, contribute to the successful delivery of the project.

Communication Barriers and Solutions

Effective communication is a cornerstone of successful project management, yet it is often fraught with barriers that can impede the flow of information and hinder project progress. These barriers can be broadly categorized into linguistic, psychological, cultural, and physical obstacles, each requiring specific strategies for mitigation.

Linguistic barriers arise from differences in language proficiency and terminology. In multinational project teams, varying levels of language skills can lead to misunderstandings and misinterpretations. Jargon and technical language further complicate communication, often alienating members who may not be familiar with industry-specific terms. To overcome these barriers, project managers should promote the use of clear, simple language and ensure that all team members have access to language support resources, such as translation tools or language training.

Psychological barriers are rooted in individual perceptions and emotions, including stress, anxiety, and preconceived notions. These barriers can distort message reception and lead to resistance or disengagement. Project managers can address psychological barriers by fostering an inclusive and supportive environment that encourages open dialogue. Regular feedback sessions and team-building activities can help build trust and reduce anxiety, allowing team members to communicate more effectively.

Cultural barriers stem from differences in cultural norms, values, and communication styles. In diverse project teams, these differences can lead to misinterpretations and conflicts. For instance, varying attitudes towards hierarchy and authority can affect how messages are conveyed and received. To mitigate cultural barriers, project managers should cultivate cultural awareness and sensitivity within the team. Providing cultural competency training and encouraging team members to share insights about their cultural backgrounds can facilitate mutual understanding and respect.

Physical barriers, including geographical distance and technological limitations, pose significant challenges to communication, particularly in remote or distributed teams. Time zone differences and lack of access to communication technologies can delay information exchange and decision-making processes. To address physical barriers, project managers should implement robust communication plans that leverage technology to bridge distances. Video conferencing, collaborative platforms, and cloud-based tools can enhance real-time communication and ensure that all team members remain connected, regardless of location.

Moreover, the selection of appropriate communication channels is critical in overcoming these barriers. Different channels, such as emails, meetings, or instant messaging, suit different types of information and urgency levels. Project managers should assess the nature of the message and the audience to choose the most effective medium for communication. Additionally, establishing clear communication protocols, including guidelines for response times and escalation procedures, can streamline communication processes and reduce the risk of misunderstandings.

In recognizing and addressing these barriers, project managers not only enhance communication but also strengthen team cohesion and project outcomes. By implementing targeted strategies and fostering an environment conducive to open and effective communication, project managers can navigate the complexities of modern project environments, ensuring that all stakeholders are aligned and informed. As project environments continue to evolve, the ability to identify and surmount communication barriers remains a vital skill for project management professionals.

Chapter 9:

Risk Management Strategies

Identifying Potential Risks

In the realm of project management, risk identification serves as a cornerstone for successful project execution. The process is not merely a preliminary step but a continuous endeavor that demands a comprehensive understanding of the project environment and its inherent uncertainties. By systematically identifying potential risks, project managers can devise strategies to mitigate adverse impacts, thereby enhancing the likelihood of achieving project objectives.

The initial phase in identifying potential risks involves a thorough examination of the project scope and objectives. This examination necessitates collaboration among stakeholders to ensure a shared understanding of project deliverables and constraints. Stakeholders, including team members, clients, and suppliers, offer diverse perspectives that are invaluable in spotting potential threats that may not be immediately apparent.

Utilizing a structured approach, such as a risk breakdown structure (RBS), aids in categorizing risks into manageable segments. The RBS organizes risks into hierarchical levels, starting from broad categories such as technical, financial, operational, and external risks, down to more specific subcategories. This organized framework facilitates a systematic review of each risk category, ensuring a comprehensive identification process.

Brainstorming sessions and workshops are effective techniques for gathering insights from various stakeholders. These collaborative sessions foster an environment where participants can openly discuss uncertainties and potential threats. The use of techniques like the Delphi method, where experts provide feedback anonymously, can also be instrumental in minimizing bias and encouraging candid assessments.

Incorporating historical data and lessons learned from previous projects is another critical component in risk identification. Analyzing past projects can reveal patterns and common risk factors that may recur. This historical perspective allows project managers to anticipate similar issues and proactively implement preventive measures.

Moreover, scenario analysis plays a pivotal role in identifying potential risks. By envisioning various scenarios, both positive and negative, project managers can identify potential deviations from the planned course and the risks associated with these deviations. This forward-thinking approach equips project teams with the foresight necessary to anticipate challenges and devise contingency plans.

In addition to qualitative methods, quantitative risk assessment tools, such as Monte Carlo simulations and decision tree analysis, provide numerical insights into the likelihood and impact of identified risks. These tools allow for a more precise evaluation of risk scenarios, enabling project managers to prioritize risks based on their potential impact on project objectives.

The dynamic nature of projects necessitates an ongoing risk identification process. As projects progress, new risks may emerge, and existing risks may evolve. Regular risk reviews and updates to the risk register ensure that the project team remains vigilant and responsive to changing circumstances.

Ultimately, the identification of potential risks is not a solitary endeavor but a collaborative and iterative process. It requires a proactive mindset and a commitment to continuous improvement. By diligently identifying and assessing potential risks, project managers lay the foundation for a robust risk management strategy, thereby safeguarding the project's success amidst the complexities and uncertainties of the project landscape. This structured approach to risk identification is integral to mastering project management and achieving strategic objectives.

Risk Assessment and Prioritization

Risk management is a pivotal component in the framework of project management, serving as a safeguard against potential pitfalls that can derail a project. The process of risk assessment and prioritization entails a systematic approach to identifying, analyzing, and responding to project risks, thereby facilitating informed decision-making and strategic planning.

The initial step in risk assessment involves the identification of potential risks that could impact the project's objectives. This requires a comprehensive understanding of the project scope, context, and environment. Techniques such as brainstorming sessions, expert interviews, and SWOT analysis are employed to uncover risks that may not be immediately apparent. The goal is to compile a thorough list of potential risks, categorized by their nature, source, and potential impact.

Once risks are identified, the next phase involves a detailed analysis to evaluate the likelihood and potential impact of each risk. Quantitative and qualitative methods are employed in this analysis. Quantitative risk analysis uses numerical methods and models to estimate the probability and impact, often resulting in a risk score. On the other hand, qualitative risk analysis involves subjective assessment of risk severity, often using a risk matrix to categorize risks as low, medium, or high priority.

The prioritization of risks is crucial to ensure that resources are efficiently allocated to mitigate the most significant threats. Risks are ranked based on their probability and impact scores, with higher scores indicating higher priority. This prioritization process enables project managers to focus their efforts on risks that pose the greatest threat to project success. Once prioritized, strategies for risk mitigation are developed. These strategies may include risk avoidance, risk transfer, risk mitigation, or risk acceptance, each tailored to the specific nature and context of the risk.

Risk avoidance involves altering the project plan to eliminate the risk or its impact, while risk transfer shifts the responsibility to a third party, such as through insurance or outsourcing. Risk mitigation aims to reduce the probability or impact of the risk through proactive measures, such as implementing additional controls or safeguards. Conversely, risk acceptance involves acknowledging the risk and preparing contingency plans to address its potential impact.

Effective communication is an integral part of the risk management process, ensuring that all stakeholders are informed about the identified risks, their analysis, and the strategies in place to address them. Regular risk reviews and updates to the risk register are essential to adapt to changing project conditions and emerging risks.

In conclusion, risk assessment and prioritization are foundational elements of successful project management. By systematically identifying, analyzing, and prioritizing risks, project managers can proactively address potential challenges and ensure that resources are allocated efficiently to safeguard the project's objectives. This structured approach not only enhances the likelihood of project success but also fosters a resilient project environment capable of adapting to unforeseen changes and challenges.

Risk Mitigation Plans

In the realm of project management, risk mitigation serves as an essential pillar that underpins the stability and success of any endeavor. Projects, by their very nature, are fraught with uncertainties that can jeopardize timelines, budgets, and outcomes. It is, therefore, imperative that project managers develop comprehensive risk mitigation plans to preemptively address potential issues and maintain project integrity.

Risk mitigation plans involve systematically identifying, evaluating, and prioritizing risks, followed by the implementation of strategies to manage these risks effectively. The initial step in this process is the identification of potential risks. This requires a thorough understanding of the project scope, objectives, and environment. Techniques such as brainstorming sessions, SWOT analysis, and risk workshops are often employed to compile a comprehensive list of potential threats.

Once identified, risks must be assessed to determine their potential impact and likelihood. This evaluation is typically conducted using qualitative and quantitative methods. Qualitative assessments involve categorizing risks based on their severity and probability, often using a risk matrix. Quantitative assessments, on the other hand, employ numerical data and statistical models to predict the potential impact of risks on project objectives.

Prioritization follows assessment, where risks are ranked based on their potential impact and likelihood. This ranking enables project managers to focus their resources and efforts on the most significant risks. High-priority risks demand immediate attention and the formulation of robust mitigation strategies.

Mitigation strategies can be broadly classified into four categories: avoidance, reduction, transfer, and acceptance. Risk avoidance involves altering project plans to eliminate the risk entirely. For instance, changing a project's scope or schedule might circumvent a potential threat. Risk reduction, conversely, seeks to minimize the impact or likelihood of a risk. This could involve implementing additional safety measures or using higher-quality materials to reduce the risk of failure.

Risk transfer shifts the responsibility of managing a risk to a third party, often through insurance or outsourcing. While this does not eliminate the risk, it alleviates the burden on the project team. Lastly, risk acceptance involves acknowledging the risk and accepting its potential impact, often when the cost of mitigation exceeds the risk's potential impact.

The implementation of these strategies requires meticulous planning and coordination. It is crucial for project teams to establish clear communication channels and assign roles and responsibilities. Regular monitoring and review of risks are also vital to ensure that mitigation strategies remain effective and adapt to evolving project dynamics. This involves conducting periodic risk assessments and updating the risk register accordingly.

Ultimately, a well-crafted risk mitigation plan not only safeguards the project against unforeseen challenges but also fosters a proactive and resilient project management culture. By systematically addressing risks, project managers can enhance decision-making processes, optimize resource allocation, and ensure project objectives are met with minimal disruption. Such foresight and preparedness are instrumental in steering projects towards successful completion, even in the face of adversity. The integration of risk mitigation plans into the project management framework is, therefore, not merely a contingency measure but a strategic imperative that enhances overall project resilience and success.

Monitoring and Reviewing Risks

In the realm of project management, the continuous surveillance and assessment of risks is paramount to the successful delivery of projects. This subchapter delves into the systematic approach required to ensure that risks are not only identified but also effectively monitored and reviewed throughout the project lifecycle.

Risk monitoring and review processes are integral to maintaining project control and ensuring alignment with project objectives. These processes involve the ongoing identification, analysis, and evaluation of risks, as well as the implementation of strategies to mitigate adverse impacts. The dynamic nature of projects necessitates a vigilant approach to risk management, as risks can evolve or new risks may emerge at any stage.

To effectively monitor risks, project managers must establish a robust framework that includes the development of risk indicators, regular risk assessments, and the integration of risk management into the overall project management plan. Risk indicators serve as early warning signals, providing insights into potential deviations from the expected project outcomes. These indicators should be developed based on the specific context of the project and should encompass both qualitative and quantitative measures.

Regular risk assessments are critical to understanding the current risk landscape of the project. These assessments should be conducted at predetermined intervals and should involve a comprehensive analysis of the risks identified in the risk register. During these assessments, project teams should evaluate the effectiveness of the existing risk mitigation strategies and determine if any adjustments are necessary. This iterative process ensures that the project remains on track and that risks are managed proactively.

Integration of risk management into the project management plan facilitates a holistic approach, enabling project managers to align risk management activities with other project processes. This integration ensures that risk management is not viewed as a standalone activity but as an essential component of the project management framework. By embedding risk management into the project plan, project managers can foster a culture of risk awareness and accountability among project stakeholders.

Communication plays a crucial role in the monitoring and reviewing of risks. Effective communication ensures that all stakeholders are informed of the current risk status and any changes to the risk profile. Regular risk reporting should be established to provide stakeholders with timely and accurate information. This transparency helps in building trust and enables stakeholders to make informed decisions regarding their involvement and contributions to the project.

Moreover, the use of technology can greatly enhance risk monitoring and review processes. Advanced project management tools and software offer capabilities such as real-time risk tracking, automated alerts, and comprehensive risk dashboards, which facilitate efficient risk management. These tools enable project managers to swiftly respond to changes in the risk environment and ensure that risk information is readily accessible to all relevant parties.

In conclusion, the monitoring and reviewing of risks is a critical aspect of project management that demands a structured and proactive approach. By implementing a comprehensive risk management framework, project managers can effectively navigate the complexities of project risks, ensuring successful project outcomes and the achievement of strategic objectives. The continuous evaluation and adaptation of risk management strategies are essential to maintaining control over the project's risk profile and ensuring its alignment with the overarching goals.

Chapter 10:

Procurement and Contract Management

Procurement Planning

Procurement planning constitutes a fundamental component of project management, serving as the blueprint for acquiring the necessary goods and services required for successful project execution. This planning process involves a systematic approach to identifying project needs, determining the procurement method, and ensuring alignment with project objectives. The primary goal is to establish a reliable framework that ensures timely and cost-effective acquisition of resources.

The process begins with a comprehensive assessment of project requirements. This assessment involves a detailed analysis of the project scope, objectives, and deliverables, which helps in identifying the specific goods and services that need to be procured. It is crucial to distinguish between items that can be sourced internally and those that necessitate external procurement. This distinction aids in formulating a targeted procurement strategy.

Once the requirements are clearly defined, the next step involves selecting an appropriate procurement method. The choice of method is influenced by several factors, including the complexity of the project, the nature of the goods or services, budgetary constraints, and the timeline for project completion. Common procurement methods include competitive bidding, direct contracting, and requests for proposals (RFPs). Each method has its advantages and limitations, and the selection must align with the project's strategic goals.

Budgeting is a critical aspect of procurement planning. It involves estimating the costs associated with acquiring the necessary resources and integrating these estimates into the overall project budget. Accurate cost estimation is essential to prevent budget overruns and ensure the financial viability of the project. This requires collaboration with financial experts and stakeholders to develop a realistic and comprehensive budget that accounts for all potential expenditures.

Risk management is another key element of procurement planning. Identifying potential risks associated with the procurement process, such as supplier reliability, quality issues, and delivery delays, is vital for mitigating their impact. Developing a risk management plan that includes contingency measures and alternative sourcing options enhances the project's resilience and adaptability to unforeseen challenges.

Supplier selection is an integral part of the planning phase. It involves evaluating potential suppliers based on criteria such as reliability, quality of goods or services, cost-effectiveness, and past performance. Establishing robust evaluation criteria ensures that the chosen suppliers align with the project's quality and performance standards. Additionally, establishing clear communication channels and fostering strong relationships with suppliers can enhance collaboration and facilitate smoother procurement processes.

Legal and contractual considerations also play a significant role in procurement planning. Drafting comprehensive contracts that clearly outline the terms and conditions of purchase, delivery schedules, and payment terms is crucial for safeguarding the interests of all parties involved. Legal experts are often consulted to ensure compliance with relevant laws and regulations and to address any potential legal issues.

Effective procurement planning requires continuous monitoring and evaluation. This involves tracking the progress of procurement activities, assessing supplier performance, and making necessary adjustments to the procurement strategy. Regular reviews and feedback mechanisms help in identifying areas for improvement and optimizing the procurement process.

In essence, procurement planning is a strategic endeavor that necessitates meticulous attention to detail, proactive risk management, and collaborative efforts among project stakeholders. Its successful implementation contributes significantly to achieving project objectives within the stipulated timeframes and budgetary constraints.

Vendor Selection and Contracts

The process of selecting the appropriate vendor is a critical component in project management, especially when the success of the project hinges on external partnerships. The complexity of modern projects demands that project managers employ a systematic approach to vendor selection to ensure alignment with project goals, timelines, and budget constraints. This subchapter delves into the methodologies and considerations involved in this crucial decision-making process, offering insights into best practices and common pitfalls.

Criteria for Vendor Selection

When selecting a vendor, project managers must first establish a set of criteria that aligns with the project's specific needs. These criteria often include the vendor's technical capabilities, financial stability, reputation, and past performance. Additionally, the vendor's ability to meet deadlines and deliver quality products or services is paramount. The importance of these criteria can vary depending on the project, necessitating a flexible yet structured approach to evaluation.

Evaluation Methods

A comprehensive evaluation often begins with a Request for Proposal (RFP) process, which provides vendors with a detailed description of the project's requirements. This process not only clarifies expectations but also allows for a comparative analysis of potential vendors. Evaluative techniques such as weighted scoring models can be employed to objectively assess each vendor against the established criteria. These models assign scores based on the degree to which each vendor meets the criteria, facilitating a quantitative comparison.

Negotiation and Contractual Agreements

Once a vendor is selected, the negotiation phase begins. This stage is crucial in establishing a mutually beneficial relationship. Effective negotiation requires a deep understanding of the project's requirements and the vendor's capabilities. The goal is to reach an agreement that satisfies both parties and lays a solid foundation for collaboration. Key elements of negotiation include price, delivery schedules, payment terms, and the scope of work.

The resulting contract must be comprehensive, clearly outlining the responsibilities of each party. It should include detailed specifications of the deliverables, performance metrics, and the criteria for acceptance. Additionally, the contract should address risk management strategies, including contingencies for potential issues such as delays or non-compliance. Clear terms regarding intellectual property rights, confidentiality, and dispute resolution are also essential to protect the interests of both parties.

Managing Vendor Relationships

After the contract is signed, the focus shifts to managing the vendor relationship. Maintaining open lines of communication is vital to ensure that both parties remain aligned throughout the project lifecycle. Regular meetings and progress reports can help identify and address any issues before they escalate. It is equally important to foster a collaborative environment that encourages transparency and trust.

Effective vendor management involves continuous monitoring of the vendor's performance against the agreed-upon metrics. Project managers must be prepared to enforce contractual obligations if necessary, but should also recognize and reward vendors for exemplary performance. Building a strong, positive relationship with vendors can lead to long-term partnerships that benefit future projects.

In conclusion, vendor selection and contract management are integral to the success of project management. By adopting a systematic approach to these processes, project managers can mitigate risks, ensure project deliverables are met, and establish a foundation for successful collaboration with vendors.

Contract Administration

Effective contract administration is pivotal to the successful execution of project management. It encompasses a comprehensive array of activities that ensure compliance with contractual obligations, facilitate communication between parties, and mitigate risks associated with potential disputes. The core objective is to maintain a harmonious relationship among stakeholders while safeguarding the project's interests.

Initially, the foundation of contract administration is laid during the drafting phase. Clear, concise, and comprehensive contract documents are imperative. They must delineate the scope of work, timelines, deliverables, payment structures, and performance metrics. This clarity minimizes ambiguities and sets a precedent for all ensuing activities.

Once contracts are executed, the focus shifts to monitoring and controlling. This involves meticulous tracking of progress against the stipulated terms. Regular audits and reviews ensure that all parties adhere to agreed-upon specifications. Deviations are promptly addressed through formal change management processes, which necessitate a collaborative approach to modify contracts without compromising the project's integrity.

Communication is a critical component. It is essential to establish robust channels and protocols for information exchange. This ensures that all stakeholders are informed of developments, potential issues, and resolutions. Regular meetings, status reports, and documented correspondence form the backbone of effective communication strategies. These practices foster transparency and trust, which are vital for maintaining positive working relationships.

Risk management is another integral aspect of contract administration. Identifying potential risks early and implementing mitigation strategies can prevent costly disputes and delays. This includes ensuring compliance with legal and regulatory requirements, which may vary significantly across regions and industries. Proactive risk assessment and management can avert potential conflicts and facilitate smoother project execution.

Furthermore, performance evaluation is crucial in contract administration. It involves assessing the performance of all parties against the contract requirements. Key performance indicators (KPIs) and benchmarks are established to objectively measure progress and quality. Performance reviews should be conducted regularly, with feedback mechanisms in place to address any deficiencies promptly. This not only helps in maintaining standards but also provides opportunities for continuous improvement.

In the event of disputes, contract administration provides a framework for resolution. Dispute resolution mechanisms, such as mediation, arbitration, or litigation, are outlined in the contract to address conflicts efficiently. It is essential to approach disputes with a solution-oriented mindset, aiming to resolve issues amicably and preserve professional relationships.

Finally, contract closeout marks the culmination of contract administration. This phase involves verifying that all contractual obligations have been met, finalizing payments, and ensuring that all documentation is complete and accurate. A thorough closeout process not only confirms the project's completion but also provides valuable insights and lessons learned for future endeavors.

In essence, contract administration is a dynamic and ongoing process that demands diligence, attention to detail, and effective communication. By adhering to these principles, project managers can navigate the complexities of contract management, ensuring that projects are executed efficiently and successfully within the agreed parameters.

Closing Procurements

In the realm of project management, the closure of procurements represents a pivotal phase that ensures the completion and fulfillment of contractual obligations. This stage is fundamental, as it signifies the formal conclusion of procurement activities, thereby safeguarding the project's integrity and financial health.

The process of closing procurements is multifaceted, encompassing several critical activities. Initially, it involves a comprehensive review and verification of all deliverables to ascertain that they meet the agreed-upon specifications and quality standards. This verification process is essential to confirm that the supplier or contractor has fulfilled their obligations as stipulated in the contract.

Following the verification of deliverables, project managers must engage in meticulous documentation. This involves compiling all relevant records, such as invoices, receipts, and correspondence, to create a comprehensive procurement file. This documentation serves as a historical record that can be referenced in future projects or audits, providing insights and lessons learned that can enhance procurement strategies.

Additionally, closing procurements necessitates the resolution of any outstanding claims or disputes. This may involve negotiation and mediation to settle any discrepancies or disagreements that have arisen during the project. Successfully resolving these issues is crucial to maintaining positive relationships with suppliers and ensuring that no legal or financial liabilities persist.

An integral aspect of procurement closure is the formal acceptance and sign-off by the client or project sponsor. This acceptance signifies their satisfaction with the deliverables and the completion of the procurement process. It is a critical step that provides assurance to all stakeholders that the procurement activities have been executed successfully and in accordance with contractual terms.

Financial reconciliation is another key component of closing procurements. This involves ensuring that all payments have been made, and any financial discrepancies are addressed. Proper financial closure not only prevents budget overruns but also ensures that the project remains within its financial parameters.

The final step in the closure of procurements is the evaluation of supplier performance. This involves assessing the supplier's adherence to timelines, quality of deliverables, and compliance with contractual obligations. The insights gained from this evaluation can inform future supplier selection processes, contributing to improved procurement efficiency and effectiveness.

Throughout the closure process, communication plays a vital role. Effective communication with all stakeholders, including team members, suppliers, and clients, is essential to ensure transparency and mutual understanding. By keeping all parties informed, project managers can facilitate a smoother closure process and foster trust and collaboration.

In essence, the closure of procurements is not merely a procedural formality but a strategic activity that reinforces the project's success. It requires a systematic and diligent approach to manage the complexities involved and to ensure that the project concludes on a positive note. By adhering to best practices and maintaining a focus on quality and compliance, project managers can achieve successful procurement closures that contribute to the overall success of the project.

Chapter 11:

Monitoring and Controlling Projects

Performance Measurement Techniques

Performance measurement is a pivotal aspect of project management, offering a means to quantitatively and qualitatively assess the progress and success of a project. It provides project managers with critical insights into whether the project's objectives are being met within the predefined constraints of time, cost, and quality.

Central to performance measurement is the concept of Key Performance Indicators (KPIs). KPIs are specific, measurable metrics that are directly linked to the strategic goals of the project. They serve as benchmarks for evaluating the effectiveness of project execution. Examples of KPIs include schedule variance, cost variance, and earned value, each offering a distinct perspective on project performance.

Schedule variance (SV) and cost variance (CV) are foundational metrics in project management. SV measures the difference between the planned and actual progress of a project in terms of time. A positive SV indicates that a project is ahead of schedule, while a negative SV suggests delays. CV, on the other hand, compares the budgeted cost of work performed to the actual cost incurred. A positive CV denotes cost savings, whereas a negative CV implies budget overruns.

Earned Value Management (EVM) is a comprehensive technique that integrates scope, schedule, and cost parameters to assess project performance and forecast future performance. EVM provides a unified view of project progress and is instrumental in identifying potential issues early, allowing for timely corrective actions. Through metrics such as the Cost Performance Index (CPI) and Schedule Performance Index (SPI), EVM quantifies cost efficiency and schedule efficiency, respectively.

The Cost Performance Index (CPI) is calculated as the ratio of earned value to actual cost. A CPI greater than one indicates that a project is under budget, while a CPI less than one suggests cost overruns. The Schedule Performance Index (SPI), on the other hand, is the ratio of earned value to planned value. An SPI greater than one signifies that a project is ahead of schedule, whereas an SPI less than one denotes delays.

Beyond traditional metrics, qualitative performance measurement techniques are gaining prominence. These techniques focus on assessing stakeholder satisfaction, team dynamics, and the quality of deliverables. Surveys, interviews, and focus groups are commonly used to gather qualitative data, providing a more nuanced understanding of project success.

Furthermore, modern project management increasingly leverages technology to enhance performance measurement. Advanced analytics, real-time dashboards, and predictive modeling tools offer dynamic insights into project performance, enabling proactive decision-making. These tools facilitate the continuous monitoring of KPIs, allowing project managers to swiftly adapt to changing circumstances and maintain alignment with project goals.

Incorporating a balanced scorecard approach can also be beneficial in performance measurement. This approach extends beyond traditional financial metrics to include customer satisfaction, internal processes, and learning and growth dimensions, offering a more holistic view of project performance.

Ultimately, effective performance measurement requires a blend of quantitative and qualitative techniques, tailored to the specific context of the project. By systematically tracking and analyzing performance data, project managers can ensure that projects are delivered successfully, meeting or exceeding stakeholder expectations while adhering to constraints.

Change Management Processes

In the realm of project management, change management processes are pivotal in ensuring that projects not only meet their intended goals but also adapt to evolving conditions and stakeholder expectations. The dynamic nature of projects necessitates a structured approach to managing changes efficiently and effectively. This subchapter delves into the various components and methodologies employed in change management within the context of project management.

Change management processes begin with the recognition of the need for change. This recognition can stem from various triggers, including shifts in market conditions, technological advancements, regulatory changes, or insights gained from project performance data. A critical aspect of this initial phase is the comprehensive assessment of the potential impact of proposed changes on the project's scope, schedule, cost, and quality.

Once the need for change is identified, the next step involves the formulation of a change request. This formal document outlines the nature of the proposed change, its justification, and the anticipated impact on the project. The change request serves as a crucial communication tool, ensuring that all stakeholders are informed and aligned regarding the change proposal.

Following the submission of a change request, a rigorous evaluation process ensues. This evaluation is typically conducted by a change control board (CCB), comprising key project stakeholders and subject matter experts. The CCB assesses the feasibility, risks, benefits, and implications of the proposed change. This stage is critical in ensuring that only changes that align with the project's strategic objectives and constraints are approved.

Upon approval of a change request, the implementation phase commences. This phase necessitates meticulous planning and execution to integrate the change into the project seamlessly. It often involves updating project documents, revising schedules, reallocating resources, and communicating the change to all stakeholders. Effective implementation hinges on robust coordination and communication among project team members.

An integral component of change management processes is the monitoring and control of implemented changes. This involves tracking the change's progress and impact on the project's overall performance. Regular status reports and performance metrics are employed to ensure that the change is delivering the expected outcomes without adverse effects on other project elements.

Throughout the change management process, communication remains a critical element. Clear and continuous communication with stakeholders fosters transparency and builds trust, facilitating smoother transitions and minimizing resistance to change. Stakeholders must be kept informed of the rationale for changes, the benefits they bring, and the progress of their implementation.

The final aspect of change management processes involves capturing lessons learned. As changes are implemented and monitored, valuable insights are gained that can inform future projects. Documenting these lessons contributes to the organization's knowledge base, enhancing its change management capabilities over time.

In conclusion, change management processes are integral to the successful execution of projects. By providing a structured framework for identifying, evaluating, implementing, and monitoring changes, these processes enable project teams to navigate the complexities of modern project environments effectively. Mastery of change management processes is, therefore, essential for project managers seeking to deliver projects that are both resilient and adaptable to change. This mastery ensures that projects remain aligned with organizational goals, even in the face of uncertainty and evolving external conditions.

Issue Tracking and Resolution

In the complex landscape of project management, the identification and resolution of issues are pivotal to ensuring the seamless progression of a project. This subchapter delves into the systematic approach required to track and resolve issues, thereby minimizing disruptions and optimizing project outcomes.

The initial step in effective issue tracking is establishing a robust framework for identification. This necessitates the creation of a comprehensive log where all project issues are meticulously recorded. Each entry should include a detailed description, categorization, and prioritization based on the potential impact on the project timeline, budget, and scope. The use of standardized templates and digital tools can significantly enhance the accuracy and accessibility of this log, facilitating real-time updates and collaboration among team members.

An essential aspect of issue tracking is the assignment of responsibility. Each logged issue should be assigned to a specific team member or subgroup, ensuring accountability and focused attention. This assignment should consider the expertise and availability of the assignee, thereby aligning the issue with the most suitable resources for resolution. In addition, setting clear deadlines for resolution is critical, promoting a sense of urgency and maintaining project momentum.

Regular monitoring and reporting are integral to the issue resolution process. Project managers should conduct routine reviews of the issue log, assessing the status of each entry and identifying any unresolved issues that may require escalation or additional resources. This ongoing oversight not only aids in early detection of potential bottlenecks but also fosters a proactive approach to problem-solving.

The resolution phase demands a flexible yet structured methodology. Upon identifying a viable solution, it is imperative to evaluate its feasibility in the context of the project's constraints and objectives. This involves a thorough analysis of potential outcomes, risks, and resource requirements. Once a decision is made, the implementation of the solution should be meticulously planned, with clear communication to all stakeholders to ensure alignment and support.

Furthermore, documentation of the resolution process is vital for future reference and learning. Detailed records of the issue, the steps taken to resolve it, and the outcomes achieved provide invaluable insights that can inform future projects. This documentation should be easily accessible to all team members, promoting transparency and collective learning.

A critical component of effective issue resolution is the feedback loop. After implementing a solution, it is important to solicit feedback from relevant stakeholders to assess the efficacy of the resolution and identify any residual concerns. This feedback should be systematically analyzed and used to refine the issue management process, enhancing the team's capacity to handle future challenges.

In the realm of project management, the ability to adeptly track and resolve issues is a hallmark of successful leadership. By implementing a structured approach to issue management, project managers can mitigate risks, optimize resource utilization, and ultimately drive projects to successful completion. The continuous refinement of these processes, informed by real-world experiences and feedback, ensures that teams remain adaptable and resilient in the face of evolving project dynamics.

Status Reporting

Effective status reporting is a critical component of successful project management. It provides a structured mechanism for communicating the current state, progress, and any potential challenges of a project to stakeholders. This transparency is vital for informed decision-making and maintaining alignment with project objectives.

Status reports serve several key functions in project management. Firstly, they facilitate communication among project team members and stakeholders. By providing a clear and consistent update on project status, these reports ensure that everyone involved is aware of the progress and any issues that may have arisen. This helps in managing expectations and aligning the efforts of all parties towards the common goal.

Secondly, status reports are instrumental in risk management. They allow project managers to identify potential risks early and communicate these to stakeholders. By highlighting areas of concern, project managers can initiate discussions on mitigation strategies and resource allocation. This proactive approach enables the project team to address issues before they escalate into significant problems that could derail the project.

Moreover, status reports provide a historical record of the project's progress. This documentation is valuable for future reference and serves as a learning tool for subsequent projects. By analyzing past reports, project managers can identify patterns or recurring issues and develop strategies to prevent them in future projects. This continuous improvement cycle is essential for enhancing the efficiency and effectiveness of project management processes.

The structure of a status report typically includes several key elements. A summary section provides a high-level overview of the project's current status, including whether it is on track, behind schedule, or ahead. It is followed by detailed sections outlining completed tasks, current activities, and upcoming milestones. These sections help to clearly convey the project's trajectory and any adjustments made to the original plan.

Another critical component of status reporting is the identification of issues and risks. This section should provide a clear description of any problems encountered, their impact on the project, and the proposed solutions. It is essential to be transparent about challenges to enable stakeholders to provide the necessary support or resources to address them. Additionally, the report should highlight any changes in project scope, budget, or timeline, providing justification for these changes.

Visual aids such as charts, graphs, and dashboards can enhance the effectiveness of status reports. They provide a quick and intuitive way to convey complex information, making it easier for stakeholders to grasp the current state of the project at a glance. Visuals can be particularly useful in illustrating progress against timelines, budget utilization, and resource allocation.

In summary, status reporting is a fundamental practice in project management, essential for maintaining open lines of communication, managing risks, and documenting project progress. By adhering to a structured approach and utilizing clear, concise, and transparent communication, project managers can ensure that stakeholders are well-informed and engaged throughout the project lifecycle. This not only facilitates smoother project execution but also contributes to the overall success of the organization's project portfolio.

Chapter 12:

Closing Projects Successfully

Final Deliverables and Acceptance

The culmination of any project management endeavor is the delivery of final outputs to stakeholders, an intricate process that demands precision, clarity, and meticulous documentation. This phase, often referred to as the final deliverables and acceptance stage, is pivotal in ensuring that project outcomes align with the predefined objectives and criteria established during the project's inception.

The primary objective in this stage is to verify that all deliverables meet the quality standards agreed upon in the project charter and scope statement. This involves a comprehensive review of each deliverable against the acceptance criteria, which must be explicitly documented and communicated to all relevant stakeholders. The criteria should encompass both qualitative and quantitative measures, ensuring that the output is not only fit for purpose but also meets the stakeholders' expectations in terms of functionality, usability, and performance.

A critical component of this stage is the conduct of a formal acceptance process. This process typically involves the project team, stakeholders, and, in some cases, third-party evaluators.

The procedure begins with the presentation of deliverables, during which the project team provides evidence of compliance with the agreed-upon requirements. This evidence may include test results, prototypes, user manuals, and other supporting documentation that substantiate the project's adherence to the specified standards.

Stakeholder engagement is crucial during the acceptance process, as it ensures that feedback is gathered and addressed in a timely manner. Effective communication channels must be established to facilitate dialogue between the project team and stakeholders, allowing for the resolution of any discrepancies or issues that may arise. It is essential to maintain transparency throughout this process, providing stakeholders with regular updates and access to pertinent information.

Once the deliverables are formally presented, stakeholders are tasked with evaluating them against the acceptance criteria. This evaluation is typically conducted through a series of tests, inspections, and reviews, designed to confirm that the deliverables fulfill the project's objectives. It is imperative that this evaluation is thorough and unbiased, as stakeholder approval is contingent upon the successful completion of this assessment.

Upon successful evaluation, stakeholders provide formal acceptance of the deliverables, which is documented through an acceptance sign-off. This sign-off signifies the stakeholders' approval of the project's outputs and marks the official transition of deliverables from the project team to the stakeholders. This transition often includes a transfer of knowledge and resources, ensuring that stakeholders are equipped to manage and utilize the deliverables effectively.

However, in instances where deliverables do not meet the acceptance criteria, corrective actions must be initiated. This may involve rework, additional testing, or modifications to the deliverables. It is crucial to address these issues promptly to avoid project delays and ensure stakeholder satisfaction.

The final deliverables and acceptance stage is a testament to the project's success, embodying the culmination of collaborative efforts and meticulous planning. It is a definitive phase that encapsulates the essence of project management, where the realization of objectives is validated through stakeholder approval, paving the way for the project's transition to its operational phase.

Project Closure Checklist

The culmination of any project necessitates a systematic approach to ensure all facets are meticulously addressed. A structured project closure checklist serves as a vital instrument, providing a comprehensive framework to verify the completion of all project activities and deliverables, ensuring nothing is overlooked in the final stages. This methodical process is crucial to affirm the project's success and to glean valuable insights for future endeavors.

Firstly, the confirmation of deliverables is paramount. It is essential to ensure that all project deliverables have been completed and meet the designated quality standards. This involves a thorough review against the initial project objectives and acceptance criteria. Any discrepancies or outstanding issues should be resolved in collaboration with stakeholders to secure their satisfaction and formal acceptance.

Secondly, the completion of administrative tasks is a critical component of the closure process. This includes finalizing all project documentation, such as project plans, schedules, and reports, ensuring they are archived appropriately for future reference. Additionally, contracts with vendors and third-party suppliers must be reviewed and closed, with all financial obligations settled. This ensures all legal and financial aspects are concluded, mitigating potential liabilities.

Resource release is another significant aspect of project closure. Human resources, equipment, and facilities allocated to the project should be systematically released. Personnel should be reassigned according to organizational needs, and any rented or borrowed equipment should be returned. This step not only optimizes resource utilization but also facilitates a seamless transition to subsequent projects.

An analysis of project performance is indispensable during closure. Conducting a comprehensive evaluation of project outcomes against the initial objectives provides insights into areas of success and those requiring improvement. This analysis should encompass a review of the project timeline, budget adherence, quality of deliverables, and stakeholder satisfaction. Such evaluations are pivotal for refining project management methodologies and enhancing future project execution.

Furthermore, the documentation and dissemination of lessons learned constitute an integral part of the closure process. This involves compiling insights gained throughout the project lifecycle, highlighting challenges encountered and strategies employed to overcome them. Sharing these lessons within the organization fosters a culture of continuous improvement and equips future project teams with valuable knowledge.

Lastly, a formal project closure meeting with key stakeholders is essential. This meeting serves as a platform to present the project outcomes, acknowledge contributions, and address any final queries or concerns. It also provides an opportunity to celebrate achievements and reinforce stakeholder relationships, laying a foundation for future collaboration.

The project closure checklist is not merely a procedural formality but a strategic component of project management. By ensuring thorough completion of all project elements, it enhances organizational knowledge, optimizes resource allocation, and strengthens stakeholder relations. Adopting a comprehensive closure checklist not only signifies the successful conclusion of a project but also contributes to the ongoing development of project management practices within the organization. Ultimately, it is an indispensable tool that ensures both the immediate and long-term success of project endeavors.

Lessons Learned and Documentation

In the realm of project management, the systematic capture and analysis of lessons learned serve as vital components that contribute to the continuous improvement of processes and outcomes. This process of reflection and documentation not only supports the enhancement of future projects but also fosters a culture of learning within the organization.

The lessons learned process commences with a thorough analysis of the project lifecycle, identifying both successful practices and areas that necessitate improvement. This analysis involves the collection of data from various stakeholders, including team members, clients, and suppliers. It is imperative to approach this gathering of information with an open mind, ensuring that all perspectives are considered to provide a comprehensive understanding of the project's execution.

Once the data is collected, it is essential to categorize the insights into actionable lessons that can be applied to future projects. These categories may include aspects such as project planning, risk management, stakeholder engagement, and resource allocation. By organizing the information in a structured manner, project managers can easily reference these insights and apply them to analogous scenarios.

To ensure the efficacy of lessons learned, it is crucial to integrate these insights into the organizational knowledge base, often through a centralized repository. This repository serves as a dynamic resource that can be accessed by project managers and team members alike, promoting the dissemination of knowledge across the organization. Furthermore, regular updates to this repository guarantee that it remains relevant and reflective of the latest project experiences.

The documentation process plays a pivotal role in institutionalizing the lessons learned. Comprehensive documentation involves not only the recording of the lessons themselves but also the context in which they were derived. This includes detailing the project scope, objectives, challenges encountered, and strategies employed. Such documentation ensures that future project teams can fully comprehend the circumstances under which the lessons were learned, thereby enhancing their applicability.

The role of documentation extends beyond the lessons learned process, encompassing all facets of project management. Accurate and detailed records are indispensable for maintaining transparency, accountability, and compliance with regulatory requirements. Moreover, well-maintained documentation facilitates effective communication among stakeholders, providing a clear and consistent narrative of the project's progress.

Incorporating documentation standards and best practices into the project management framework is essential for achieving consistency and quality in record-keeping. This may involve the adoption of standardized templates, checklists, and guidelines that ensure uniformity across all projects. Regular training and awareness programs can further reinforce the importance of meticulous documentation among project teams.

Ultimately, the lessons learned and documentation processes are intertwined elements that collectively contribute to the refinement of project management practices. By fostering a culture of continuous learning and maintaining robust documentation, organizations can enhance their project delivery capabilities, mitigate risks, and achieve sustained success. The integration of these processes into the organizational fabric not only enhances individual project outcomes but also strengthens the overall strategic objectives of the organization.

Celebrating Success

In the realm of project management, the attainment of project goals is a testament to the rigorous application of methodologies and the collaborative synergy of the team. Recognizing and celebrating these achievements is not merely an act of acknowledgment but a strategic component that reinforces positive outcomes and motivates future endeavors.

Project completion is often seen as a culmination of efforts, where objectives have been met within the constraints of time, resources, and scope. However, the true value lies in comprehensively analyzing the success factors that contributed to the project's fruition. This analysis provides insights into best practices, innovative problem-solving, and effective risk mitigation strategies that can be applied to future projects.

Celebrating success in project management involves a systematic evaluation of the project's lifecycle. This begins with a detailed review of the project plan and execution phases, assessing the alignment with predefined goals and the adaptability of the team to dynamic challenges. It is crucial to identify the key performance indicators (KPIs) that were achieved and understand the variables that influenced their attainment. Such an evaluation fosters an environment of continuous improvement and learning, essential for sustainable success.

Furthermore, recognizing individual and team contributions plays a significant role in maintaining high morale and fostering a culture of excellence. Acknowledgment can be executed through formal recognition programs, awards, or informal gatherings that highlight the efforts and dedication of team members. This not only boosts team spirit but also cultivates a sense of belonging and commitment to the organization's objectives.

Strategically, celebrating project success can enhance stakeholder relationships. By transparently communicating the outcomes and impact of the project, stakeholders are reassured of the project's value and the team's capability to deliver. This transparency builds trust and confidence, essential for garnering support in future initiatives. Moreover, documenting success stories and case studies serves as a powerful tool for showcasing the organization's competencies and achievements to external partners and clients.

Incorporating feedback from all project stakeholders is another critical element of celebrating success. Engaging stakeholders in post-project evaluations provides a holistic view of the project's impact and uncovers areas for potential improvement. This inclusive approach ensures that diverse perspectives are considered, leading to more robust and informed decision-making in subsequent projects.

The role of leadership in celebrating success cannot be overstated. Leaders are instrumental in setting the tone for recognition and appreciation. By actively promoting a culture that values success and learns from challenges, leaders empower their teams to strive for excellence. Leadership should also facilitate opportunities for team members to share their experiences and insights, fostering a collaborative and innovative environment.

In essence, celebrating success in project management is a multi-faceted approach that combines evaluation, recognition, communication, and leadership. It is an integral part of the project lifecycle that not only acknowledges achievements but also lays the groundwork for future success. Through understanding and embracing the elements that contribute to project success, organizations can cultivate a resilient and motivated workforce, ready to tackle future challenges with confidence and expertise.

Chapter 13:

Advanced Topics and Trends in Project Management

Agile and Scrum Methodologies

Agile methodologies, a paradigm shift in project management, emerged in response to the limitations of traditional, linear approaches. Characterized by iterative development, customer collaboration, and responsiveness to change, Agile methodologies prioritize adaptability and efficiency. Central to this approach is the Agile Manifesto, a set of principles advocating for individuals and interactions over processes and tools, working software over comprehensive documentation, customer collaboration over contract negotiation, and responding to change over following a plan.

Scrum, an Agile framework, is widely adopted due to its simplicity and effectiveness. It structures work in iterations known as sprints, typically lasting two to four weeks, during which a potentially shippable product increment is developed. The Scrum framework comprises key roles, events, and artifacts that facilitate collaboration and productivity.

The Scrum Team, fundamental to the framework, includes the Product Owner, Scrum Master, and Development Team. The Product Owner is responsible for maximizing the product's value by managing the Product Backlog, a dynamic list of tasks and requirements. The Scrum Master serves as a facilitator, ensuring adherence to Scrum practices and removing impediments to progress. The Development Team, composed of cross-functional professionals, is tasked with delivering increments of the product during each sprint.

Scrum events structure the workflow and ensure alignment among team members. The Sprint Planning meeting initiates each sprint, where the team collaborates to select Product Backlog items for completion and formulates a Sprint Goal. Daily Scrums, brief stand-up meetings, provide a platform for team members to synchronize efforts, discuss progress, and address obstacles. The Sprint Review, held at the end of each sprint, involves stakeholders and offers an opportunity to inspect the product increment and adapt the Product Backlog as necessary. The Sprint Retrospective, a final event, allows the team to reflect on the sprint and identify areas for improvement.

Artifacts in Scrum, such as the Product Backlog, Sprint Backlog, and Increment, provide transparency and focus. The Product Backlog is a prioritized list of features, enhancements, and bug fixes, continuously refined by the Product Owner. The Sprint Backlog, a subset of the Product Backlog, includes tasks committed to during Sprint Planning. The Increment represents the sum of all completed Product Backlog items and must meet the Definition of Done, a shared understanding of completion criteria.

The Agile and Scrum methodologies offer numerous advantages, including enhanced flexibility, improved product quality, and increased stakeholder engagement. By promoting iterative development and fostering communication, these methodologies enable teams to respond effectively to changing requirements and market conditions. However, successful implementation requires a cultural shift, embracing collaboration, transparency, and continuous improvement.

In conclusion, Agile and Scrum methodologies represent a transformative approach to project management, prioritizing adaptability and stakeholder value. By understanding and implementing these frameworks, organizations can achieve greater efficiency and deliver superior products. As the business landscape continues to evolve, Agile and Scrum methodologies remain indispensable tools for navigating complexity and driving innovation.

Project Management Software

In the intricate landscape of contemporary project management, the integration of specialized software has emerged as a pivotal component in enhancing efficiency, accountability, and collaboration. As projects grow in complexity and scope, the demand for robust and adaptable project management software becomes increasingly critical. These digital tools are designed to streamline processes, manage resources effectively, and facilitate communication among diverse teams across various geographical locations.

The core functionalities of project management software typically encompass task assignment, scheduling, resource allocation, and progress tracking. Through a centralized platform, project managers can assign responsibilities, set deadlines, and monitor the status of individual tasks. This visibility ensures that all team members are aligned with the project's objectives and timelines, thereby reducing the risk of miscommunication and delays.

One of the significant advantages of employing project management software is its ability to provide real-time data analytics. By leveraging these capabilities, project managers can make informed decisions based on current metrics and trends. This data-driven approach allows for the identification of potential bottlenecks, resource constraints, and performance issues, enabling proactive measures to mitigate risks.

Furthermore, project management software often includes features such as Gantt charts, Kanban boards, and dashboards, which offer visual representations of the project's progress. These tools facilitate a comprehensive understanding of the project's status at a glance, aiding in the effective management of timelines and deliverables. The ability to visualize the project roadmap and its components fosters a strategic overview that is essential for successful project execution.

Collaboration is another critical aspect enhanced by project management software. In today's globalized work environment, teams are frequently dispersed across different regions and time zones. Software solutions provide a platform for seamless communication and collaboration, allowing team members to share documents, discuss ideas, and provide updates in real time.

This integration reduces the silos that often hinder productivity and ensures that all stakeholders are engaged and informed.

Resource management is another area where project management software excels. These tools enable project managers to allocate resources efficiently, ensuring that human, financial, and material resources are utilized optimally. By tracking resource utilization, managers can identify underutilized assets and reallocate them to areas of need, maximizing the project's overall efficiency and effectiveness.

Security and data integrity are paramount in the digital age, and project management software vendors have responded with robust security measures. Features such as user authentication, data encryption, and access controls ensure that sensitive project information remains secure and confidential. This trust in the security of the software allows organizations to focus on project execution without concerns about data breaches or unauthorized access.

As technology continues to evolve, project management software is expected to integrate more advanced features, such as artificial intelligence and machine learning algorithms. These advancements will further enhance predictive analytics, automate routine tasks, and provide deeper insights into project performance. Adopting and adapting to these innovations will be essential for organizations aiming to maintain a competitive edge in project management.

In essence, project management software serves as an indispensable tool in the modern project manager's arsenal, offering a comprehensive suite of functionalities that drive project success through enhanced collaboration, data-driven decision-making, and efficient resource management.

Sustainability in Project Management

The integration of sustainability into project management has emerged as a critical innovation, reshaping the traditional paradigms of project execution. This evolution is not merely a response to environmental concerns, but also an acknowledgment of the broader societal and economic implications of project activities. The application of sustainable practices within project management requires a multifaceted approach, encompassing environmental stewardship, social responsibility, and economic viability.

Environmental stewardship involves minimizing the ecological footprint of a project throughout its lifecycle. This can be achieved through the adoption of green technologies, efficient resource utilization, and waste reduction strategies. Projects are increasingly being designed with a focus on energy efficiency, renewable resources, and sustainable materials. This shift not only mitigates environmental impact but also often results in cost savings, as energy-efficient practices can lead to reduced operational expenses.

Social responsibility in project management emphasizes the importance of considering the impacts on local communities and stakeholders. Projects must be developed with an awareness of their potential social consequences, ensuring that they contribute positively to the community. This may involve engaging with local stakeholders to understand their needs and concerns, and incorporating these insights into project planning and execution. Socially responsible projects are more likely to receive community support, which can facilitate smoother implementation and reduce the risk of conflicts.

Economic viability, the third pillar of sustainability, requires projects to be financially sound while delivering long-term value. This involves not only managing budgets and timelines effectively but also ensuring that the benefits of the project extend beyond immediate financial gains. Projects should be assessed for their potential to contribute to economic development, such as job creation and infrastructure improvement, which can enhance the overall economic fabric of the region.

To effectively integrate sustainability into project management, practitioners must adopt a holistic perspective, considering the interdependencies between environmental, social, and economic factors. This requires a shift from traditional linear project management approaches to more dynamic, systems-thinking methodologies. Project managers must be equipped with the skills to identify and manage sustainability-related risks and opportunities, ensuring that projects are resilient and adaptable to changing conditions.

In practice, this integration involves setting clear sustainability objectives at the onset of a project, which are aligned with broader organizational goals and values. These objectives should be measurable and monitored throughout the project lifecycle, using key performance indicators that reflect the project's sustainability impact. Regular assessment and reporting on these indicators can drive continuous improvement and accountability.

Moreover, fostering a culture of sustainability within project teams is crucial. This involves training and empowering team members to make decisions that support sustainable outcomes, and encouraging innovation and creativity in problem-solving. Collaboration across disciplines and sectors can also enhance sustainability efforts, as diverse perspectives can lead to more comprehensive and effective solutions.

The incorporation of sustainability into project management not only addresses the pressing challenges of our time but also offers a pathway to more resilient and successful projects. By balancing environmental, social, and economic considerations, project management can contribute to a more sustainable future, achieving outcomes that are beneficial for all stakeholders involved.

Future Trends and Innovations

In the ever-evolving landscape of project management, emerging technologies and methodologies are reshaping traditional paradigms. As organizations strive for greater efficiency and adaptability, the integration of innovative tools and approaches becomes paramount. One of the most significant trends is the adoption of Artificial Intelligence (AI) and Machine Learning (ML) in project management processes. These technologies facilitate predictive analytics, enabling project managers to anticipate potential risks and resource constraints with greater accuracy. AI-driven tools can automate routine tasks, such as scheduling and data analysis, allowing managers to focus on strategic decision-making and stakeholder engagement.

Another transformative trend is the increasing reliance on Agile and hybrid methodologies. Agile, with its iterative and flexible approach, has proven effective in managing complex projects where requirements are dynamic. However, the hybrid model, which combines Agile with traditional Waterfall methods, is gaining traction as it offers the best of both worlds—agility and structure. This approach allows project teams to adapt to changing conditions while maintaining a clear roadmap and timeline.

The rise of remote work and distributed teams is another critical factor influencing project management practices. The global pandemic accelerated the shift towards virtual collaboration, necessitating the adoption of digital tools and platforms to facilitate communication and coordination. Cloud-based project management software has become indispensable, providing real-time access to project data and enabling seamless collaboration across geographies.

Sustainability and social responsibility are increasingly becoming integral to project management. As organizations recognize their environmental and social impacts, projects are being designed with sustainability in mind. This shift is not only about reducing ecological footprints but also about ensuring projects contribute positively to society. Project managers are now tasked with balancing economic goals with environmental stewardship and social equity.

The integration of Internet of Things (IoT) and Big Data analytics is also reshaping project management strategies. IoT devices provide real-time data that can be used to monitor project progress and performance. Big Data analytics, on the other hand, allows for better decision-making by identifying patterns and trends that may not be apparent through traditional analysis methods. These technologies enable a more proactive approach to managing projects, reducing the likelihood of unforeseen issues and enhancing overall project outcomes.

The human aspect of project management is also undergoing transformation. As automation takes over routine tasks, the focus shifts to developing soft skills such as leadership, communication, and emotional intelligence. These skills are crucial for managing diverse teams, navigating complex stakeholder landscapes, and fostering an inclusive work environment.

Lastly, cybersecurity is becoming a critical consideration in project management. With the increasing digitization of project data, ensuring the security of sensitive information is paramount. Project managers must work closely with IT departments to implement robust cybersecurity measures and educate team members on best practices to protect against data breaches.

As these trends continue to evolve, project managers must remain adaptable and open to learning. Continuous professional development and staying abreast of technological advancements will be essential to navigate the future of project management successfully. The integration of these innovations promises not only to enhance efficiency and effectiveness but also to redefine the role of project managers in a rapidly changing world.